# *The Biblical Shape of Hope*

**Ralph L. Murray**

**BROADMAN PRESS**
*Nashville, Tennessee*

To Two Colleagues—
One of Whom
Opened to me the door of hope, and
The Other of Whom
Encouraged me by his help
To walk on through

ISBN: 0-8054-1122-4

Library of Congress Catalog Card Number: 79-143283
Dewey Decimal Classification: 220.8
Printed in the United States of America

# *Foreword*

A danger exists in reducing anything to its essence—if, indeed, that can ever be done. But at risk of running that danger, permit me to attempt in the beginning to find place for the word "hope" in our Christian vocabulary.

Ever since Paul, as rediscovered by Martin Luther and other reform theologians, we evangelicals have ascribed (perhaps unwittingly) to what Carl Braaten has called a "theology of glory." Such a theology centers in the cross of Jesus, making the cross the crux of theology. An emphasis like that is not unfaithful to the New Testament, but it does want balancing.

For the habit of theologians (and preachers) who center on the glory of the cross is to claim too much for man and man's accomplishments. Braaten describes the tendency well: "Such a thought [the glory of the cross] leads to ecstacies of fulfilment in theology, knowing too much (gnosticism) in the church, claiming too much (triumphalism) in religion, pretending too much (perfectionism) for the times in which we live."[1]

As a preacher friend of mine put it, describing a sister (and competitive) preacher and congregation: "Over there they sing: 'Would you be free from your passion and pride?' But at our place, we know we are still plagued with both

---

[1] Carl Braaten, *The Future of God* (New York: Harper & Row, 1969), p. 83.

passion and pride, so we sing: 'Through many dangers, toils, and snares, we have already come.'"

That contrast, cast in the familiar mold of hymns we all regularly sing, puts nicely the necessity for that balance which the hope of the resurrection has put in our total emphasis.

For the truth is, we still smart—even though in Christ—under the burden of our sin and mortality. There is a glory in the redemption Christ brings, but the redemption has a "not yet" aspect to it. Resurrection and hope speak to and inform that "not yet" of our here and now.

In these chapters, an attempt has been made to color and enrich the landscape of hope. If you were to think of hope as a beautiful gem, refracting its light spectrum in different colors and vibrations according to the vantage point taken, you would have something of the concept of this little book. It invites you to hold the shimmering gem of hope up to the light of certain biblical characters and ideas, daring to believe that by so doing you will become more grateful that "we have this hope."

One last closing admission. These thoughts are not uniquely mine. My own concepts have been enriched from many sources. However, I take sole responsibility for the way they appear here. The writing of these chapters is my work; not the work of my colleagues. Nor is it the work of the leadership of the Sunday School Department, nor, indeed, of the Sunday School Board.

Ralph L. Murray

# Contents

# 1

## *Hope as Anchor*

### Hebrews 6:19-20*a*

Billy Graham, in a sermon titled "The Climax of History," pointed up a climate that exists among some of our current philosophers: "Pessimism about life is the prevailing mood of many of our intellectuals today," he said. And then Dr. Graham continued: "In his essay, *A Free Man's Worship,* Bertrand Russell writes: 'All the labors of the ages, all the devotion, all the noonday brightness of human genius, are destined to extinction in the vast death of the solar system.' The soul's habitation, he says, is nothing 'but unyielding despair.' An equally well-known thinker, H. G. Wells, wrote in his closing years a book entitled *The Mind at the End of Its Tether.* He declared, 'The end of everything we call life is close at hand and cannot be evaded.' The philosopher Will Durant thinks that it is 'impossible any longer to believe in the permanent greatness of man or to give life a meaning that cannot be annulled by death.' "[1]

We would do well to ask, Why this dark despair? Is this the prevailing mood of those who reflect upon the meaning of our common existence? Perhaps you already know something about these men: their beliefs; their way of life. If so, then you already have made the mental note that each man is a non-Christian. Perhaps earlier they had professed a belief that gave reason to hope. But if so, despair had not yielded to that belief nor that hope. And perhaps, with Richard Wagner, they had come to think that by abandoning hope altogether, it would be possible to rid one's self of

---

[1] *Decision,* January, 1965, pp. 1,14.

despair.[2] But if that was their tactic, it misfired. Despair was the end they came to anyway.

But, you would *not* be wrong were you to make the mental reservation: these were intellectuals. Most of *us* are not that. We would be more inclined to accept the sentiment of Quixote in *The Man from La Mancha* when he admitted to being an idealist because "I have never had the courage to believe in nothing." Yet not all those who have managed to keep despair at arms' length stand on identical ground. Some are *groundless optimists*. The sheer force of their life's vital juices has delivered them from despair. They have learned to discipline themselves, not admitting themselves to the dubious luxury of pessimism. Such optimism may not be a virtue. It is a desirable trait. Who cannot but be warmed by any who can see the happier part? So we take to our hearts the little girl who, when her circus balloon burst upon a rock, could say to her mother, "Well, I still have the stick." Some people seem to have glands that dispose them to cheerfulness. But about those fortunate people we are not thinking here.

Nor are we thinking of anticipation—the momentary diversion—by which life is made tolerable. Psychologists say we all need to have pleasant interludes to look forward to. Someone has said that when there is no hope for the future there is no power in the present. Have you ever faced some unpleasant, even dreaded, experience by anticipating some pleasurable and palatable experience lying just beyond the pain? So we endure a trip to the hospital, a trip to the dentist, surgery, pain, and sustained stress in the power of an anticipated joy. Such devices for coping are not unnatural or undesirable. But anticipation of that order is not Christian hope—our topic here. We have in mind a dynamic,

---

[2] See quote of R. Wagner in letter to Friederich Nietzsche in Edward J. O'Brien, *Son of the Morning: A Portrait of Friederich Nietzsche* (New York: Brewer, Warren & Putnam, 1932), p. 122.

a power, an energy tougher and more durable than that.

Our topic here is Christian hope. Now Christian hope is, obviously, for those persons who hold a certain kind of religious belief. About them, the writer of Hebrews noted: "Which hope we have as an anchor of the soul, both sure and stedfast, and which entereth into that within the veil; whither the forerunner is for us entered, even Jesus, made an high priest for ever after the order of Melchisedec" (Heb. 6:19-20).

This particular kind of hope—the hope I hold and that holds me—can better be shared if we seek to understand it: What it is, and what it is not. To that end, let me propose three ways of looking at Christian hope. First, we shall examine the basis of hope: faith. Then, we will turn to the earnest of hope: the Spirit. And at the last we shall survey briefly hope's goal: salvation.

## 1. Faith: The Basis of Hope

Faith is the foundation of hope; the ground out of which hope rises. But what is faith? The writer of Hebrews suggested an answer to that question which sounds a bit like double-talk: "Now faith is the substance of things hoped for, the evidence of things not seen" (Heb. 11:1). Then he illustrated his definition with the citation of a series of heroes and heroines—some of whom we shall look to later in relation to our theme of hope.

When one backs off and thinks about all these heroes and heroines, looking for some common denominator, one characteristic seems to emerge into sharp focus. They were men and women of action. But more, they acted on the basis of a religious belief. They are cited by the writer of old as having faith. He substantiates his claim in terms of that which they did because of their faith. Or to say the same thing another way, the heroes and heroines of Hebrews 11 were motivated by religious belief.

Further clarification of that religious belief is given in verse 6: "But without faith it is impossible to please him; for he that cometh to God must believe that he is, and that he is a rewarder of them that diligently seek him." Apparently their faith began with a belief in God. It continued with an action, or series of actions, based on a belief in what God would do in response *to their action*.

Now if you will turn that Scripture sentence found in Hebrews 11:6 over in your mind for a moment, it may dawn on you—as it has me—that the holy writer of old opened an insight on to faith that we might otherwise miss: namely, faith is a choice. Think of it this way. Imagine one has come to a crossroads, and out of the two possibilities, he has to make a choice. In this case, the choice is to believe in God or not believe in God. If we were to use the language of the theologian or the philosopher, we would say that our imaginary man (the hero of faith) has chosen *theism* in preference to *atheism*. So we have come upon the *subjective* aspect of faith.

But faith is more than mere subjective choice. Once our imaginary traveler has made his choice, he begins to travel that way. He chooses to believe in God, and that belief imposes upon him certain constraints; certain ways of responding to life. And in the response, a new element of faith appears. The assumption (which we have called choice) of faith is confirmed by experience. And in the confirmation of faith's assumptions, springs hope. Such confirmation of faith and the rise of hope would be an *objective* aspect of faith.

But faith has more objective evidence to offer than the confirmation of our belief; our assumptions about God and his nature. Peter has a sentence in which he names an objective basis for faith, linking hope with faith as faith's offspring. Here is that sentence: "Blessed be the God and Father of our Lord Jesus Christ, which according to his abundant mercy hath begotten us again unto a lively hope by the resurrection of Jesus Christ from the dead, to an inheritance incorruptible, and undefiled, and that fadeth not away, reserved in heaven for you, who are kept by the power of God through faith unto salvation ready to be revealed in the last time" (1 Pet. 1:3-5).

Now in that rather long sentence Peter has named an objective basis for faith. Were I to put his truth in my own words, I think it could be made a simple declarative sentence: *We can believe God because of the resurrection of Jesus Christ.* Moreover, the early apostolic church offers further evidence of that truth by her very life: She was the community of hope created by the fact of the resurrection. So Alan Richardson can write: "The Resurrection of Christ is God's mightiest act; it has created our faith; and it is, as it were, an eschatological symbol in history of our ultimate salvation and therefore the ground of our hope."[3] In fact, the resurrection of Jesus defines both our hope and our future, as John saw: "We shall be like him; for we shall see him as he is" (1 John 3:2).

And if faith be the ground of our hope, we may add that behind faith is choice to commitment. In the deepest possible sense, the sensitive Studdert Kennedy saw this truth, and expressed it with a poignant beauty:

> I bet my life on Beauty, Truth,
> And Love, not abstract but incarnate Truth,
> Not Beauty's passing shadow, but its Self.
> It's very self made flesh, Love realized.
> I bet my life on Christ—Christ Crucified.
>
> . . . . . . . . . . . . . . . . . . . . . . . . . . . . . . . . . . . . . . . . . . . . . .
> . . . Through the clouds of Calvary—there shines

---

[3] *A Theological Word Book of the Bible* (New York: The Macmillan Co., 1960), p. 109.

His face, and I believe that Evil dies,
And God lives on, loves on, and conquers all.

. . . . . . . . . . . . . . . . . . . . . . . . . . . . . . . . . . . . . . . . . . . . . . . .

. . . Such is my Faith, and such
My reasons for it, and I find them strong
Enough. And you? You want to argue? Well,
I can't. It is a choice. I choose the Christ.[4]

I would amend that witness, so that it would read: "I choose
the God who has disclosed himself in the Christ." When one
has done that, he has a basis for hope.

## 2. The Spirit: The Earnest of Hope

The nature of hope is to take for evidence the unseen,
according to our biblical definition. That is, we have to turn
the wisdom of the marketplace inside out: Not, "seeing is
believing" but "believing is seeing."

"Believing is seeing"—but not right away. Often hope
must suffer the contradiction of circumstance. So Abram
hoped for a city, but lived in a tent. When he got to the land
he took for the fulfilment of the promise, he found a
"famine in the land" (Gen 12:10). Paul hoped to preach
the gospel in Rome, but when he arrived in that imperial
city, he was Nero's prisoner. Hope's vision is often obscured
by seeming contradictions.

And is it not strange how little of trouble can shake, and
even rattle our hope? Perhaps hope is so fragile because it
is so undernourished. Harry Emerson Fosdick once wrote a
sentence we need to ponder: "In the crises of life . . . our
words show where our souls have been feeding."[5] Perhaps,
given better nurture through prayer, worship, and service,
our hopes would be more sure. For trouble cannot rattle the

---

[4] G. A. Studdert Kennedy, *The Unutterable Beauty* (London: Hodder
& Stoughton, 1964 paperback edition), pp. 16-17.

[5] *The Beam,* December, 1965, p. 16.

hope of a true Christian. On the contrary, hope grows stronger under stress. Do you recall how Paul traced out the contrapuntal dynamics of constricting circumstances and expanding hope?

"Now that we have been put right with God through faith, we have peace with God through our Lord Jesus Christ. He has brought us, by faith, into the grace of God in which we now stand. We rejoice, then, in the hope we have of sharing God's glory! And we also rejoice in our troubles, for we know that trouble produces endurance, endurance brings God's approval, and his approval creates hope. This hope does not disappoint us, for God has poured out his love into our hearts by means of the Holy Spirit, who is God's gift to us" (Rom. 5:1-5, TEV).

God's gift to the hope he has created in us through Christ, while living under the contradiction of constricting circumstance, is his Spirit. Through the Spirit, restricting circumstance has the effect of expanding hope. In Romans 8, Paul detailed how the process works out in life. Under the contradictions of life, the Christian's hope endures and waxes stronger. The Spirit firms us in our infirmities, even assisting us in praying as we ought. Morover, the Spirit confirms in us the unspeakable comfort that life's seeming contradictions of hope are blessings God gives with his left hand; that nothing in life, or in death, or in the universe may separate us from God, who holds us in his steadfast love through Christ.

A good test for any truth is to ask: How does it do in the face of our ultimate contradiction of hope: the threat of death? Would you admit one man's testimony? W. Cosy Bell was a teacher of young ministerial students in a mountain preacher's training school. When in middle life he learned that he was about to die from cancer, he sent a message to his boys. That message rings with the confidence of an expanding hope caught in the center of constricting circumstance: "I've grown surer of God every year of my life, and

I've never been so sure of him as I am right now. I'm glad
to find that I haven't the least shadow of shirking or un-
certainty . . . I've been preaching and teaching those things
all my life, and I'm so interested to find that all we've been
believing and hoping is so."[6]

How could Cosy Bell be so certain? Long ago, he had
chosen to believe the God revealed in Christ, and all his
life's action since had followed out of that choice. In his
life's unfolding God had confirmed his choice with the gift of
the Spirit, who had nurtured hope in him; a hope that ex-
panded while his life on this planet constricted. And so, for
Cosy Bell, hope had not been confounded—even by the
spectre of death. Is that not what the apostle Paul meant
when he exulted: "For I am persuaded, that neither death,
nor life, nor angels, nor principalities, nor powers, nor things
present, nor things to come, nor height, nor depth, nor any
other creature, shall be able to separate us from the love of
God, which is in Christ Jesus our Lord" (Rom. 8:38-39).

### 3. Salvation: The Goal of Hope

Thus far we have seen that hope rests on faith; is nurtured
by God's indwelling Spirit. There remains hope's goal.

Perhaps we can understand the importance of hope's goal
better by way of illustration. In the days of the Irish potato
famine of 1846, as part of the relief program, men were put
to work building a road which had no purpose whatever. It
was simply a device to give men work to do. From that
background, Gerald Healy, in his play *The Black Stranger,*
has Michael come home to his father, and say with a kind
of poignant despair: "They're making roads that lead to
nowhere!"[7]

---

[6] Ralph L. Murray, *From the Beginning* (Nashville: Broadman
Press, 1964), p. 128.

[7] William Barclay, *The Mind of St. Paul* (New York: Harper & Bros.,
1958), pp. 229-230.

But hope does better than that; infinitely better. Hope's goal has a personal and a cosmic dimension. The personal goal—resurrection—has already been assured by the resurrection of our Lord. The cosmic redemption is linked with our personal redemption. How? He who is Lord of death is also Lord of creation. As creation innocently participated in man's fall—as a means toward man's judgment—so the whole cosmos will participate in man's redemption—as an evidence of God's power. The redemption of the creation is necessary; evil and good cannot coexist eternally. So in Romans 8, the apostle Paul traces out the sequence: "All of creation waits with eager longing for God to reveal his sons. For creation was condemned to become worthless, not of its own will, but because God willed it to be so. Yet there was this hope: that creation itself would one day be set free from its slavery to decay, and share the glorious freedom of the children of God" (Rom. 8:19-21, TEV).

So we have this hope! Let us suppose, assuming for a moment the darkest of all possibilities, that this hope, rooted in faith, certified by the Spirit, confirmed in our own experience, is after all, groundless. What then? What have we lost in this life? And my answer is: "Nothing. I have lived a full life; a life of purpose and meaning. I have lost nothing that I really needed or wanted."

But—since we have dared to look at the darkest of all possibilities—it is only fair that we turn the question around. Suppose my hope is true, as God is true. What then? What have I gained? And my answer is: "Everything. I have all this, and heaven too!"

No wonder the early Christians used the anchor as the symbol of their hope, often in company with the sign of the fish. And the writer of Hebrews, seeking to lay hold of every positive reinforcement for the faith of beleaguered Christians, took hold of that familiar symbol to express the sure ground of the Christian's hope: "Which hope we have as an anchor

of the soul, both sure and stedfast, and which entereth into
that within the veil; whither the forerunner is for us entered,
even Jesus, made an high priest for ever after the order of
Melchisedec" (Heb. 6:19-20). Perhaps you noticed how
hope, in the argument of the holy writer, merged into the
figure of Christ, already entered behind the veil and into the
presence of God.[8] What was the inspired writer saying? Let
me set before you what I think he was saying, and you test
it for truth. "Hope is not our anchor; our anchor is Christ.
Our future, out of which hope comes to us as God's gift, is
with Christ. Indeed, Christ himself is our future, and without him, we have no future and no hope. But, because we
have Christ, we have this hope."

---

[8] See T. H. Robinson, *The Epistle to the Hebrews,* The Moffatt Com-
mentary (London: Hodder & Stoughton, 1946), pp. 88-89.

# 2

## *Hope as Movement*

### Genesis 12:1-3; Hebrews 11:8-10; Romans 5:1-5

John Steinbeck has observed a restlessness that he says marks Americans, and has described it: "A burning desire to go, to move, to get under way, anyplace, away from Here." He has talked with Americans, too, and says that he has discovered that in their talk the idea of movement dominates: "They spoke quietly of how they wanted to go someday, to move about, free and unanchored, not toward something, but away from something."[1]

Perhaps you noticed that last descriptive phrase: ". . . not *toward* something, but *away* from something." If that be true, then in that phrase is the pathos of a movement without hope.

Our chapter title suggests, however, that movement is a shape of hope. As a matter of fact, hope may have early expressed itself in the Bible through movement. But if so, then that movement has a particular kind of quality; a quality which we may even designate as the "shape" of hope. And it is about that movement that we concern ourselves here, seeking (as we do) the various biblical shapes of hope. In this chapter we shall see hope as movement, and with these distinguishing marks: direction, derivation, and deferment.

### *1. Hope's Direction*

Steinbeck spoke of the American's movement as "away

---

[1] John Steinbeck, *Travels With Charley, In Search of America* (New York: Viking Press, 1962), p. 10.

from something." If that be true, then we need to ask: "Away from what?" If we could know the answer to that question, then perhaps we might know our own errant moods better. We do—at times—have this uneasy suspicion; this impulse to run away; this urge to escape. But is where we are so bad that anywhere else promises to be better? And by the way, are we thinking geographically of the soil or of the soul?

Sometimes a people tells on itself by the songs it sings or has others sing. The top ten tunes can be an accurate barometer of those subterranean depths of our existence that we dare not surface. With that in mind, one of the recent top ten tunes is quite interesting. The recurrent question of the song is a haunting, "Is that all there is?" You may recall the story only hinted at in the lyrics. First, the little girl, watching from the street as her home burns down in the dead of night, responds to those first intimations of the tragic and waste that is in life with her question, "Is that all there is?" Later the exciting promise of the circus proves more than the reality of elephants and painted clowns. Reflecting on how much pleasure promises and how little pleasure gives, the little girl asks in almost pathetic disbelief, "Is that all there is?" Still later, the little girl, now grown-woman, tastes of the cup of a friendship blossomed into love, only to have that relationship ruptured by a death (whether of life or love we are not told). Out of the instinct of loss and hurt, the child-grown-woman asks again, "Is that all there is?" Then someone suggests to her (according to the song) that if life is so grievous, perhaps it is not worth the living. Her reply, you will recall, is that though life is empty, she will exhaust it, and then repeats the refrain (which has been sung after each raising of the basic question): "If that's all there is, then let's keep on dancing; let's break out the booze, and have a ball."

Now that was a top tune for weeks on end. The lyrics, the

plaintive strain, the noetic poignancy—all of it caught the fancy of Americans. It reflected accurately a mood, a stance of the American spirit. And in that song we told on ourselves and about ourselves. We confessed we had lost any sense of direction. If we had any movement (we admitted), it was movement away from, not to. "Is that all there is?" was a confession of a bankruptcy of the spirit; an innocent way of admitting that meaning had been wrung out of life for many. The song describes motion with no arriving; circles with no direction.

Now, interestingly enough, Abram was a man on the move, as was his father Terah before him. We may well ask if Abram differed in any significant way from the girl in the sad song. To answer, we need to recover a memory of his beginnings. The record contains an obscure hint that Abram may have suffered, along with his father, a crisis of meaning. A clue, and nothing more than that, may lie in the apparently innocent coincidence that Abram's trek from Ur, and from Haran, began after a death in the family. First, it was the death of Abram's brother, Haran. Shortly after, Abram and Terah moved out. Significantly enough, when they have stopped, the name of the place is Haran—the dead brother's name. Then later, it was the death of Abram's father. Was it the old restlessness returned? Was Abram running away from something?

We can only guess what may have been the root of the movement. But when the community of faith looked reverently back upon Abram's movements, they saw something more significant than flight from harsh life. They tell us that Abram was running *to* something, and in words like these: "Now the Lord had said unto Abram, Get thee out of thy country, and from thy kindred, and from thy father's house, unto a land that I will shew thee: And I will make of thee a great nation, and I will bless thee, and make thy name great; and thou shalt be a blessing" (Gen. 12:1-2).

But more than that, the movement of Abram is explained in terms of his earliest hope: "For he looked for a city which hath foundations, whose builder and maker is God" (Heb. 11:10). Does that not indicate direction? But more, does not that movement indicate hope? So we come here upon the first shape of hope in the Bible: movement. And hope, when it is an active force, gives a man's movement direction.

## 2. Hope's Derivation

But if hope gives a man's movement direction, then we are driven back one thought-step to ask a question about so impelling a force in human behavior: What is the basis of hope? Or, we could put the question another way: Out of what does hope spring? Again, we look at Abram. The same Hebrews passage we noted before informs us that Abram's movement was caused (at bottom) by faith; faith in God. Drawn on by hope, Abram was sustained in the day-to-day stress of his trek by faith. The writer of Hebrews sets forth in one sentence the whole dynamic: "He believed that God is, and that he is the rewarder of them that diligently seek him." In that sentence is an understanding of hope's derivation.

We would, however, probably be in error if we were to conclude that such a faith was easy to come by, even for Abram. Much of the evidence in Abram's world ran against the kind of faith to which he opened himself. There was in Abram's world, for example, a veritable cornucopia of affluence and cultural stimulation that any alert, vital man would be loathe to leave. Abram did not come upon the scene at the dawn of human achievement. On the contrary, his city of Ur was the repository of a rich heritage reaching back seven times farther than the United States (as a political entity) is old. Bright, an expert on such matters, has written a couple of sentences that has put Abram's time in a perspective we may not have thought about before:

"In Mesopotamia, by the age of Israel's origins, a whole tide of civilization had flowed and ebbed; Sumerian culture had come into being, run a magnificent course of over fifteen hundred years, and finally played itself out. Israel was born into a world already ancient."[2]

That Ur had a civilization already ancient may come as a kind of surprise. More surprising, though, may be the kind of technology that civilization had managed to bring off. It rivaled the urban societies of our own day, except perhaps, in noise and air pollution. Hear a description of the world which was Abram's and which he was willing to leave:

> This was a period of great urban development in the course of which Mesopotamian civilization was given normative form. The system of dykes and canals which made intensive cultivation of the alluvial plain possible was by this time fully developed. Population increased apace and great cities sprang up everywhere; city-states, where they did not already exist, were developed . . . . The great temple complex in Warka (Erech) [exhibits] features characteristic of Mesopotamian temple architecture through all centuries to come. Everywhere new techniques are in evidence. The wheel, and ovens for firing pottery, were in use, making possible a ware of great technical excellence. Processes for pounding, then for pouring copper were developed. Exquisite cylinder seals, which replace the earlier stamp seals, attest a rare artistic development.[3]

To leave all that for what the modern song calls "the impossible dream"—what would possess a man? We can only imagine, but imagination offers a possibility. Could it be that Abram had learned that a man's life is of a different order

---

[2] John Bright, *A History of Israel* (Philadelphia: The Westminster Press, 1959), p. 36. Used by permission.
[3] Ibid., p. 23.

than things? And did this mean cutting across the grain of popular theological thought, current in Mesopotamia? The "going thing" theologically, so far as we can tell, was to tie in with the gods of the city-state that had everything going their way. Affluence and religion went hand in hand. Even the gods fared according to the Gross National Product! Bright explains, ". . . A god's prestige rose or fell with that of the city in which he had his residence."[4] That being true, Abram cut across the grain of his time with a god who looked like a loser. The only city Abram's God had was the El Dorado of Abram's hope.

But even so, Abram may have come to a crisis of meaning. Like Kipling's McAndrews of a more innocent time than now, he saw (or perhaps felt) the crisis coming:

> We're creepin' an wi' each new rig—less weight and
>     larger power;
> There'll be the loco-boiler next an' thirty knots an' hour,
> Thirty an' more; what I hae seen since ocean steam
>     began
> Leaves me nae doot for the machine: but what aboot
>     the man?[5]

Modern man, if that were Abram's mood, can identify. He has clawed his way to the top of a mountain of impressive achievements. And these achievements have been coming with accelerated pace. One scientist I heard lecture had condensed the history of life on earth to one calendar year, and the timetable went something like this: man had appeared on the scene December 31, four hours before midnight. Social life had appeared one hour before; civilization one minute prior; Christ had come 30 seconds before; the secret of the atom had been broken less than one second in

---

[4] Ibid., p. 59.
[5] Rudyard Kipling, "McAndrews Hymn," T. S. Eliot, *A Choice of Kipling's Verse* (New York: Charles Scribner's Sons, 1943), p. 58.

the past." And in these last split seconds of geologic time, man has been feverishly busy. While the industrial revolution lasted nearly 500 years, the atomic age lasts but eleven. And from Sputnik (Oct. 4, 1957) to Christmas, 1969, man had spiralled his space technology into a trip to the moon.

Now the spiritual impact of all this on modern man may be put in one sentence: Man has a tendency to become his own godlike hero. And this is not difficult to understand. Earlier man had lived under the rigors of certain built-in limitations, all of which were accepted as a part of the human condition. Any authentic human being had to submit to at least these: the necessity of hard labor; the inevitability of disease and tragedy; the brutal whimsey of unpredictable nature; the stark fact of death—usually at an early age.

With such an insidious array of powers against him, man found comfort in the idea of a Higher Power, who was above life and nature, and who—though his ways were inscrutable—still held out to man the intimation that he might (by faith) join up with the winning side. Man, in this frame of reference, saw himself as a kind of "amphibious" creature: belonging to the present world, but also identifying with this Higher Power (usually called God) who gave him identity with another world which was to come. To be human was to recognize (as a matter of realism) the dimension of the tragic in life, but it was also to live (through faith) in hope.

From Abram until recent times this was man's natural stance: between the two worlds, belonging to both while groaning under the curse of this one, but daring to hope for deliverance to the perfect world that was yet to be. But now, man the heroic achiever has "come of age" (to use Bonhoeffer's phrase). Let Professor Keen describe the con-

---

" Lecture at Union Seminary, New York, by Dr. Harold Schilling, Dean of the Graduate School and Professor of Physics, Pennsylvania State University.

tradiction of this man, supposedly emancipated by his
cunning inventiveness, but still caught in the web of his
finitude:

> It would not be too extravagant to say that the funda-
> mental thesis of the new view of man which is coming
> to dominate the 20th century intellectual is that modern
> man has become posthuman. To be a "modern man" is
> to recognize that one is discontinuous with traditional
> man. It is to join in the refrain "Nothing like us ever
> was." Somehow, because we belong to the 20th century,
> we are supposed to be freed from the limitations that
> governed past human beings and also to be incapable of
> believing in the reality of anything that transcends the
> testimony of sense and experience.[7]

Modern man, on the midway of his technological carnival,
finds it difficult to go against the theological grain of his
time. Belief for him is as hard to come by as it was for
Abram. But come we must, if we are to hope. The role of
superhero must be abdicated; mortality must be admitted;
death, tragedy, and waste must be taken as a part of the
essential mystery of our world and the life that is. For the
question of God is not about the existence of some remote
being. It is the question of the possibility of hope. If God
is really dead, then death is God, and Dante's inscription
might well be inscribed over all life: "Abandon hope, all ye
who enter."

So Abram may have found hope hard to come by. But to
have no hope was even harder. So—out of the sheer pressure
of his humanity—Abram "believed that God is, and the
rewarder of them that diligently seek him." To say that about
Abram, or any man, is to say that he has found the ground
for hope.

---

[7] Sam Keen, "Hope in a Posthuman Era," Marty & Peerman, *New
Theology No. 5* (New York: The Macmillan Co., 1969), p. 82.

### 3. Hope's Deferment

Perhaps all the way through up until now, you have been bothered by a little untidiness of analogue. Is "shape" movement? Or is it form? The word "shape" seems to imply fixed form. Movement, however, is not fixed. It is dynamic. Can, then, *movement* describe the "shape" of hope?

Yes, if "shape" is thought of as dynamic. What, for example, is the shape of our social structures? At any one point in time you might be able to describe the relationships and structures of our society, but even while in the process of describing, the shape may be changing. I am writing while the postal workers are on strike. Who can say that the description I give to the form of our postal service (its shape) as presently structured will be the shape of that service when you read these lines? Shape, in that sense, is dynamic.

And in that dynamic sense, the shape of hope is movement. Not only is the movement of hope the movement of the *one* who hopes (such as Abram's movement from Ur and Haran), but hope itself is subject to changed form. Could we see this in Abram's experience?

When Abram left Haran, the form for his hope was "a city which has foundations, whose builder and maker was God." At the beginning, Abram's hope had the shape of some spiritual El Dorado. But Abram never found that city; his hope in that form was never realized. Yet hope did not die; hope changed in form. Abram exchanged (somewhere in the gradual accumulation of wisdom in the pilgrimage) his hope for a city to a hope for a seed (Gen. 15:2). From a city to a seed; that movement speaks both of hope's deferment and through deferment to hope's changing shape. For hope rises out of us; out of our felt needs. With Abram, the felt need may have been the crisis of meaning, precipitated by death—the death first of his brother; then his father. But the shape of his hope was influenced by the world and the gods Abram knew. Since the Sumerian gods were identified with the city-states in the Sumerian culture, Abram's hope took on the shape of the "city which has foundations."

Yet, in time and under the pressure of experience, Abraham's hope changed shape (as we have noted): from a city to a seed. The movement of hope (in terms of its more significant shape) represents a spiritual growth that came through disappointment, testing, and frustration. For all the while Abram looked for that city, he lived in tents, enduring famine, wars, family conflicts and all the rest. But since the nature of hope is to rise out of what we are (and are becoming), it is in the nature of hope to change. And when hope is refined, hope reflects some deepening spiritual currents in the life. As Abraham came to know more about this God whom he had come to believe in (a knowledge which was faith confirmed through experience), his hope changed. From a city to a seed. This was the movement of hope itself: a movement toward refinement.

When one reflects on the import of Abraham's pilgrimage, and the changed shape of his hope, he is challenged to examine the shape of his own hope. Does the shape of one's hope suggest a self-centered spirit? One that seeks nothing but that which enhances himself and his own future? Or has hope's shape been refined so that he looks, not for a mere city, but for a seed? Not simply a new Jerusalem with streets of pure gold, but a family of God with God as Father, Christ as Elder Brother, and everyone who wills as brother and sister?

Crass hope has never known this kind of movement. Rather, it settles for a narrow, distorted vision, and squats there. So the woman in this homely little caricature:

> She even thinks that up in heaven
> Her class lies late and snores,

> While poor black cherubs rise at seven
> To do celestial chores.[8]

The fatal flaw of unrefined hope is that it betrays an entire religious stance that centers in one's self. Everything—conversion, prayer, hope, church, heaven—is thought of and described in terms of self and one's own need. But as hope is refined, hope becomes inclusive.

Perhaps you have noticed something of that in Bunyan's Pilgrim and Christiana. Pilgrim's experiences were all concerned with himself: his guilt, his salvation, his hope for the Celestial City. He never sought his seed.

In contrast was Christiana, who shared many of the same experiences as Pilgrim, and at last arrived in the Celestial City, too. But with this difference: Pilgrim arrived alone, while Christiana had her children with her. Pilgrim never got through seeking the city; Christiana sought the city for her seed. Hope, when it is refined, moves to that.

---

[8] "For a Lady I Know" from *On These I stand* by Countee Cullen. Copyright 1925 by Harper & Row, Publishers, Inc.; renewed 1953 by Ida M. Cullen. Reprinted by permission of Harper & Row, Publishers, Inc.

# 3

## *Hope as Promise*

### Genesis 28:18-22;  35:9-12;  48:3-5,15-16

When Jacob went down into Egypt, he took the promise
with him. Had it been a bank note, its value might have
been questioned. The promise was that old. All the promise
had delivered up until that fateful day was himself, a cave
at Machpelah, and his hope. All? Perhaps we had better
say it another way. Without the promise, Jacob would have
gone down to Egypt hopeless. It was the promise that kept
Jacob going, even when it meant going to Egypt. And in that
sentence we find another shape of hope: the promise.

Perhaps we ought to stop right here, and draw out the
distinction between hope and courage. Some have the nerve
and the grit to go on without hope. Even though there is
no pull of the future on them, they manage to stay up and
going. Such an one is Jean-Paul Sartre, who once confessed
of his atheism: "Atheism is a cruel and long-range affair,
never publicly flirting with hope or grace."[1] But though he
has never flirted with (nor been sustained by) hope, Sartre
has kept on bearing the burden of his freedom; kept on
writing, kept on protesting the uselessness of it all. Sartre
may have the courage life demands, but that course is not
colored by the warmth of a convincing hope.

Nor is hope mere optimism. We shall have more to say
of this later, but just now let us note this difference: optimism
fails to take into realistic account the element of the tragic
in life. Thus optimism wears out with impatience and
disillusionment after a while. Optimism, when frustrated

---

[1] From *Time*, "The Prophet of Nevertheless," October 30, 1964, p. 44.

sufficiently, may turn anarchic or even nihilistic. In contrast, hope does take realistically the tragic. And when hope is confronted by the tough powers of the Dark One, hope stays sweet and keeps on working. For while optimism has no ally beyond the human, hope looks finally to a source outside and beyond itself. Hope finally rests in God.

This difference, as you have probably already observed, issues out of hope's theology. And good theology can be a comfort, as even Charlie Brown knows. You may have seen that cartoon panel. In the first frame, Lucy and Charlie Brown peer out a window on a rainy scene. Lucy seems to be thinking out loud: "Boy, look at it rain. . . . What if it floods the whole world?" In the next frame, Charlie Brown informs Lucy of the promise in the rainbow as set forth in Genesis 9, to which Lucy replies: "You've taken a great load off my mind. . . ." Charlie Brown makes our point then: "Sound theology has a way of doing that."[2] Sound theology takes loads off, and sound theology *helps men hope* when life loads up, too.

So we observe at the outset that when Jacob went to Egypt, he took the promise with him. And that promise was the basis for his hope. Interestingly enough, that was about all the promise had given him: hope. Through a long life, the promise lingered on the borders of fulfilment, but never quite arrived. The promise was always there, and the expectation the promise generated—the hope. But nothing Jacob could nail down, tie up, and salt away. Something the promise seemed to offer was always coming loose.

How explain the durability of Jacob's hope, then? What was in his hope that disappointment, danger, and even death could not dissipate? The answers to such questions, should we find them, may strengthen our own hope; our own belief

---

[2] As taken from *Bible Society Record*, November, 1965, p. 150, Courtesy Knox Press.

in the promise. So let us look closer at Jacob under these
headings: Tentative Hope, Testing the Hope, and Hope
Tested.

### 1. Tentative Hope

Jacob heired the promise through deceit. Or so he thought.
And thinking that made the promise tentative, so far as Jacob
was concerned. You will recall that Jacob thought the promise rested on his father's blessing. But not so. The promise
rested on the character of God. That is the point the sacred
storytellers are seeking to make. When God makes a promise,
the promise is as sure as God is sure. Even man's treachery
cannot make God's purpose miscarry. But Jacob did not
know that. For Jacob the promise was tentative. And so
was the hope.

It may seem to you that Jacob's utilitarian approach to
the promise was a bit irreverent, even crass. Jacob would
use the promise, if the promise worked! How impious can
one be?

But Jacob was not irreverent; he was basically honest. Jacob
knew (perhaps unconsciously) the wellsprings of faith and
was not going to profess finally a faith that did not make
sense for him. For faith, you see, is only one category of
belief. And how can one believe in something that won't
work? Perhaps we need to take a deeper look into that
question.

Belief comes as a result of opinions formed in response to
the stimuli of our experience and environment. We have
many kinds of belief. Certain beliefs are religious, and we call
those beliefs "faith." Now the beliefs may correspond to
reality; they may not. Jacob's concern was to be sure his
belief had a responding reality. Until he could be sure, he
would regard the promise as tentative.

Perhaps we can see how this works better in a common
experience. In an excellent chapter on the intrinsic relation-

ship of belief to being, Dr. Don Harbuck cites such an experience, showing how we come to have opinions and then beliefs. In his example, Harbuck's particular concern is to differentiate between opinions and beliefs. Opinions we hold tentatively; beliefs more tenaciously. Here is the illustration:

> Driving an automobile at night after fatigue has taken its toll, you can find these distinctions clearly illustrated. You become aware of a pattern of lights down the road. Then you start forming an opinion about these lights. Your mind thumbs through the possibilities. Is this an approaching vehicle, an illuminated truck trailer, a wayside farmhouse, a road intersection? Experience has taught you that all of these are possibilities. Your consciousness collects other data and flashes them on the screen of awareness as the lights grow nearer and the reflective powers of your mind synthesize the evidence and finally develop the right "belief." Yet everyone in comparable circumstances who has embraced the wrong opinion about an object of which he was aware can discern quickly the fundamental difference between *awareness* and *belief* and *the essential nature* of each.[3]

The fact to keep in mind here is that belief may correspond to reality, or it may not. But any belief, whether valid or invalid, has the power to direct human effort. Goering's belief in Hitler and the Third Reich could be offered as evidence of the power of belief—even false belief.

Well, perhaps Jacob had a "feeling" about the promise he had heired. He was not sure of his belief in the promise or in the God who had given it. Therefore he would put that belief to the test. He would discover the reliability of the promise through experimentation. Mark you: in the be-

---

[3] Don B. Harbuck, *The Dynamics of Belief,* (Nashville: Broadman Press, 1969), pp. 14-15.

ginning, Jacob's hope was tentative. He would see if this belief were trustworthy.

## 2. Testing the Hope

Now Jacob, holding the promise and its hope as tentative, was not dissimilar from modern man, at least in one respect. He was going to put this tentative belief to the test: he was going to use the empirical method. Any high schooler can tell you about the empirical method. You are given a hypothesis, a laboratory with Bunsen burners, test tubes and a passel of chemicals, and a procedure. Then the experiment is conducted: the hypothesis is tested to see if it is true. That is the empirical method. Modern man is basically an empiricist. Jacob has this similarity to us.

Isn't that what the bargain at Luz was all about? You recall the terms: "If God will be with me, and will keep me in this way that I go, and will give me bread to eat and clothing to wear, so that I come again to my father's house in peace, then the Lord shall be my God, and this stone, which I have set up for a pillar, shall be God's house; and of all that thou givest me I will give the tenth to thee" (Gen. 28:20-22, RSV). In short, Jacob was conducting an experiment. He wanted to see if experience would confirm the reliability of the promise. Or put another way, he wanted to see if the promise meant that he could hope.

Now this must be said for Jacob: the kind of testing he proposed was strong stuff. He was carrying the promise out to real life. No ivory tower theorizing for Jacob. He wanted to know: Would it work where the action is?

If our religious beliefs are frail these days, it may be that we have not really carried those beliefs to the test. Perhaps the kind of lives we live make such tests well-nigh impossible.

In fact, we scarcely seem to need religious beliefs, as Harbuck reminds us: "A number of forces in the modern world have teamed up to shoulder formal religion to the sidelines.

Science offers explanations and provides ways of achievement that once belonged to the province of religion. These developments have seemed to leave less and less operating room for religious activity. Science as cosmology (astronomy, physics, geography, and so on) was originally the domain of religious interpretation. Medicine was the practice of the priesthood. Education was the sole prerogative of the church. Even sanitation was under the control of ceremonial laws of cleanness and uncleanness, dietary regimen, and the like. Through the processes of secularization, one of these areas after another has been reassessed and taken over by some scientific discipline. If a person can understand his world and get what he needs to *live well in it*—without reference to formal religion, why bother with church at all?"[4]

Yet, modern man does have his hang-ups; his collisions with harsh reality. Perhaps we have the advancing technologies to thank for that. One perceptive observer has described at least a part of it:

> Our culture has shifted the age of anxiety from youth to late middle age.
>
> Before the middle of this century the young were anxious about their ability to make it in a cruel, competitive society. Even the chance to get one's foot on the first rung of the ladder of success was just that—a chance to be hoped for . . .
>
> But . . . the age of personal anxiety is no longer youth, it is . . . middle age. Job security is a thing of the past. The higher the level of responsibility in business, industry, and even church positions, the greater the insecurity. The subject is taboo in polite society, but listen with the ears of your heart to the corporation executives and the pastors and their wives. Yesterday's achievements are for the history books and have no current value,

---

[4] Harbuck, op. cit.; pp. 12-13.

while a pack of well-trained, self-confident young men are pushing them to an earlier retirement.

The rapidity of change has made experience obsolete. A man's hard-won experience may be a liability rather than an asset. This is why the young, the inexperienced, and the recently educated are desired by both business and the church. How often I have heard, "He was a capable man who did his job well, but his job outgrew him.[5]

Perhaps this is a time to learn from Jacob, He took the tentative promise from Bethel to Laban's house—to a battle of wills and wits between uncle and nephew. It was raw life; rough stuff. After seven years of it, the supplanter was the supplanted: Leah was taken to the nuptial bed masquerading as Rachel. Later on, the test was more uptight: in the intimate confines of the home. Jacob contended with domestic strife, sibling rivalry, and in-law troubles. As Jacob grew in scope and power, life added the tests of intrigue, war, death, bereavement, economic reverses, and about anything else that life can conjure up to test a man and his beliefs. These were the stresses of Jacob that put the promise to the test. The design was to test the reality of the promise, and the integrity of the Promiser. One does not need to think deeply to see that Jacob in method and procedure, was akin to the modern man. He would not make these judgments about worth and belief on somebody else's say so. He had to see for himself. Like Tennyson's Arthur Hallum,

> He faced the specters of the mind
> And laid them; thus he came at length
> To find a stronger faith his own,
> And Power was with him in the night,

[5] Duke K. McCall, "The Age of Anxiety," *The Tie* (Louisville: Southern Baptist Theological Seminary), March, 1970, p. 2.

Which makes the darkness and the light,
And dwells not in the light alone.

### 3. Hope Tested

Pass over Jacob's long life. Go with him at long last to Egypt, when about all he could take was the promise. See him as he prepares to die. Was the promise worth anything then?

This we can count on: if Jacob had anything positive to say about the promise when the chill wind of death was blowing for him, then we can take it for an estimate of substance. In such a time, a man generally speaks his mind. I recall an instance of that kind of honesty. It was an epitaph on a marker looking out over the North Atlantic, hard by the Norman castle built at Abrystwyth by Edward I in 1277. The date on the marker was December 21, 1818. The name was David Davies. The confession had to be his own:

My sledge and hammer lie reclined
My bellows, too, have lost their wind;
My life extinct, my forge decayed
And in the dust my vice is laid.
My coal is spent; my iron's gone;
My nails are drove, my work is done.

That is the mood that death lays on a man. When death came near Jacob, what did he think of the promise?

Were it not for the sacred chroniclers of Israel, we might never know. But they gave us a record. According to them, the promise was worth passing on. Joseph's sons, Ephraim and Manasseh, were before the old man. And he spoke his mind about the promise: "God almighty appeared to me at Luz in the land of Canaan and blessed me, and said to me, 'Behold, I will make you fruitful, and multiply you, and I will make of you a company of peoples, and will give this land to your descendants after you for an everlasting possession.' And now your two sons, who were born to you in the land of Egypt, . . . are mine. The God before whom my fathers Abraham and Isaac walked, the God who has led me all my life long to this day, the angel who has redeemed me from all evil, bless the lads; and in them let my name be perpetuated, and the name of my fathers Abraham and Isaac; and let them grow into a multitude in the midst of the earth" (Gen. 48:3-5,15-16, RSV).

Jacob had known, in his long life, what it was to have much and little. He had been the master in his own tent, and now he was servant in the land of Pharaoh. But none of that mattered. What did matter was that he had the promise. And with the promise, he had hope. Is that not the meaning of the old man's blessing: that the promise was worth passing on? And, too, the hope that the promise carried?

# 4

## *Hope as Surprise*

### Exodus 3:1 to 4:5

Off Provincetown, Massachusetts, some years ago, a U.S. Naval submarine sank. As soon as the mishap was discovered, rescue operations were set in motion. Divers found the sub after some time, but all feared for the lives of the men trapped inside. The rescuers tapped the side of the inert behemoth of the deep, hoping against hope. Then, muffled by the pressures of the water's depth but unmistakably, there came from within the sub the sound of a gentle tapping. What message did the trapped men have for the world outside? Painful letter by painful letter the message came. It was a question: "I-S—T-H-E-R-E—A-N-Y—H-O-P-E—?

When one stops to reflect on it, the notion comes that in that question is still another shape of hope: surprise. The idea is that hope suggests the possibility of making a good thing out of that which for the moment appears to be bad; very bad. Hope implies that the ordinary course of events, suggested by our own predictive factors (which draw from our own experience and that of others), will be short-circuited. Hope implies the introduction of the unusual, the unpredictable, the more-than-human into a bad and deteriorating situation. Hope suggests surprise as a possibility.

Does this shape of hope have any biblical foundation? For an answer to that question, let me suggest that we turn to Moses, that towering figure of Old Testament salvation history. As we review his life and labors, we shall see that hope did take this shape of the unexpected, effecting a reclamation of the man himself, and of an enslaved people. Further, I hope to make it clear that hope as surprise rises out of the nature of God, who as the Supreme Innovator, can initiate new patterns in old structures thus bringing to pass some new thing. And that, we shall see, is the basis of hope as surprise.

## 1. Hope as Surprise for Moses

One would have to have been sometime in his life where Moses was at Horeb, if he would have the capacity to appreciate the miracle that emboldened Moses for hoping again. Have you ever been there? The sheer immensity of your tumbled-in world overwhelms you.

For Moses, Horeb was the backside of nowhere. He was out of his element there, like a fish out of water. He had been born and reared for better things than the boondocks. Adoptive son of Pharaoh's daughter; enriched by Egypt's finest education; sensitized to the feelings of others by his Hebrew mother—Moses must have been overwhelmed at the sheer waste his life had come to. His blundering but well-intentioned efforts on behalf of a Hebrew slave had blown the whole thing. Had he planned it out, or had he that time to go over again, he would do it differently. But time, like the river, flows on. One does not recall the past; he lives with it, mistakes and all. And in Moses' case, the mistake seemed irreparable. His past had made a fugitive out of him. Horeb was home only because he had nowhere else to go.

But what does one do when life falls in around his ears and all his skills and training count for nothing? Does he simplify life, jettisoning all excess baggage? Is it possible to pare life down to its bare essentials? To exist, if one cannot live?

Not only possible, but necessary. The only problem is that in the jettisoning, hope is likely to go. And if a man in such a situation has no future, his present cannot mean much. He lives more on instinct and reflex than on the higher drives and powers of the fulfilled and fulfilling human being. He is a man, but without a man's identity; just a living organism, moving through empty days and haunted nights. Living with what might have been, and is not.

But if a man is to survive, he has to discover that the essence of his selfhood is beyond all the trappings that were, the roles that he formerly played. Victor Frankl, the Austrian psychiatrist who survived two and a half years in four different Nazi concentration camps, came to observe that a man can endure almost any mode of life, provided he has found meaning in life. And when life falls in on a man, he discovers that if his selfhood has any meaning, that meaning is invariably related to the selfhood of his God. In that marvelously profound story of the prodigal son, you may have noticed that immediately after the son came to himself he said, "I will arise and go to my father." Could it be that his remembered relationship to the father helped him come to himself; to a sense of selfhood? Bit by bit, the man who has been broken on the wheel of life puts together the pieces of his selfhood. He restructures his relationships. And in the broken bits of life, sooner or later—if he is to survive—he makes a discovery: God is with him, always. Even in the brokenness. This was the conclusion of Dorothy Thompson after visiting Dachau and studying the records there: "They who remained men, in conditions of lowest bestiality, served an Image and an Ideal higher than the highest achievements of man."[1] Like Moses, we all have to learn that even in Horeb we belong to God.

Was Moses in some such struggle for survival down there in Horeb? We cannot know for sure. But we are sure of the subjective dimension when hope's surprise overtook him. Had you or I been at Horeb that fateful day, would we have seen the bush burning? Or was that sight reserved only for

---

[1] "Dachau," *Ladies' Home Journal,* September, 1945.

the eyes that were prepared to see? Again, we cannot speak dogmatically. But this may be a clue: the design and the art of the storyteller.

I once heard Dr. J. Hardee Kennedy of New Orleans seminary speak of the artful design of those first chapters of Exodus. You may have noted the first words of Exodus 3:1: "Now Moses." Here, in this way, we have introduced to us the subject. Not only is such a construct foreign to ordinary Hebrew syntax, but that syntax is a novel device in the story. Up until those words, the emphasis has been altogether on the action, as is usual in Hebrew storytelling. But with the words "now Moses" our attention is moved from the objective facts to the subjective actor. Could that be a hint?

The construct is the more remarkable when one casts a backward glance over the way the storyteller has brought us. There is the narrative of Israel, sinking into bondage; the birth and nurture of Moses; his rearing and education; his early concern for social justice and his abortive effort to arbitrate between the oppressed and the oppressor. When his gesture exploded in the deathblow to the Egyptian, we have the story of Moses' flight for his life from Egypt. In all this material there is a smooth flow from event to event, with no emphasis established at all. But the storyteller had his own designs: he was setting the stage for the subject. He brought us through all those introductory materials until at last he was ready for the subject. Then the chronicler wrote: "Now Moses." Moses was set on stage, front and center, bringing with him all his own particular interior furnishing that the stories related can only suggest. Whatever else we may conclude, surely this is warranted: the surprise of the burning bush was at least partially the product of all that was embraced in the man, Moses.

The burning bush—which we remember best from this classic account—"burned, but was not consumed." The fact that it was not consumed was only the beginning of surprises, however. The greater surprise for Moses was that by means of the burning bush God communicated with him, and that in that communication he had the capacity to receive and understand the message. More, he felt an inner necessity to make response. In this dialogue came the glimmerings of the dawn of new hope for Moses. All was not waste and loss. God was going to use everything that had been a part of him: his Egyptian education and status; his desert cunning, honed through these years as shepherd for Jethro; his natural sympathies for the Hebrew slaves. God was about to do a work that could only be described by the word "surprising." All God waited upon was the man's assent. Given that, hope was born and the surprises would unfold one upon another.

What does that say to the man who, like Moses, finds life tumbled in midway through his years? First, I think Moses' surprise informs us that we must be sensitive to perceive the ways in which God may be seeking to communicate with us; to surprise us with hope. Elizabeth Barrett Browning, in her "Aurora Leigh," put her finger on the failing we must always contend with:

> Earth's crammed with heaven,
> And every common bush afire with God.
> And only he who sees take off his shoes;
> The rest sit around and pluck blackberries.

Second, Moses' surprise reclamation assures us that where God and man are concerned nothing is lost, nothing is too broke to mend. In a now near-forgotten era of American politics that catapulted Richard Nixon into a national prominence that ended at the White House, one of the minor actors was a man named Whittaker Chambers. In his earlier years, Chambers had been a part of the Communist spy apparatus in the United States, and as such had helped penetrate to some of the highest councils of government. But Chambers had become disenchanted with communism and had rebuilt his life, establishing himself in a career as journalist. In this profession the former Communist had risen to the post of a senior editor of *Time* newsmagazine. In that sensitive post, Chambers was appalled to discover that one of his former Communist cellmates, Alger Hiss, had become an assistant to the Secretary of State. As such, Hiss had participated as an advisor in the decisions of Yalta and Teheran. Chambers could not bear to be silent. His witness, however, was ignored and stifled by the powerful influences of the President of the United States, acting (some believed) in narrow partisan interests. Nixon, a freshman congressman from California, befriended Chambers, giving him a congressional hearing as a setting for getting his story out to the nation. Eventually, as a result of Chambers' witness, Hiss was convicted of perjury and sent to prison. Out of that experience, in which Chambers himself was surprised by the national scope of his action, the former Communist turned patriot wrote a book in which he expressed this sense of surprise that can overtake a man who sees how God uses the particularities of his life, infusing loss and waste, pain and misunderstanding with an unanticipated meaning:

"I do not know any way to explain why God's grace touches a man who seems unworthy of it. But neither do I know any other way to explain how a man like myself— tarnished by life, unprepossessing, not brave—could prevail so far against the powers of the world arrayed almost solidly against him, to destroy him, and defeat his truth . . . I am an involuntary witness to God's grace and to the fortifying power of faith."[2] Chambers, like Moses, experienced that surprising grace of God by which—in his providence—we dare to hope.

## 2. Hope as Surprise for a People

Earlier we observed that when Jacob went to Egypt he

---

[2] Whittaker Chambers, *Witness Whittaker Chambers* (New York: Random House, 1955), p. 6.

took the promise with him. He had tested the promise and thought it worth passing on. But now 400 years have passed. The sacred writer tersely reports that there came a "new king over Egypt, which knew not Joseph" (Ex. 1:8). Some historians see a possible relationship between that line in the Bible account, and the rise and fall of the Hyksos dynasty in Egypt—the shepherd kings who had their capital at Avaris in northeast Egypt.[3] However that may be, the descendants of Jacob had fallen on hard times. They had only a dim hope that the promise had any vestige of meaning. They had nearly dismissed it as impossible.

But God had not. The burning bush experience was explained to Moses in terms of the promise wanting redemption: "I have seen the affliction of my people who are in Egypt, and have heard their cry because of their taskmasters; I know their sufferings, and I have come down to deliver them out of the hand of the Egyptians" (Ex. 3:7-8, RSV). God had his surprise for Jacob's descendants, and in that surprise lay the possibility of hope. That is to say, the descendants of Jacob came to have hope because of the nature of their God. The best in Hebrew consciousness never really got over the surprise of it, and were appalled that any could. Jeremiah was one such, who in one of his earliest messages expressed this sense of double surprise: at the marvel of what God had done and at the wonder of the people's unfaithfulness. (See Jeremiah 2:1-8.) Psalm 78 expresses astonishment at the surprising way God gave Ephraim (the northern kingdom) deliverance and hope, and at how perversely they tended to turn from that God while holding to a distortion of the hope he had given them. Jeremiah, the psalmist, and others never ceased to be surprised at what God had done, and in their surprise they found reason for hope.

[3] John Bright, *A History of Israel* (Philadelphia: The Westminster Press, 1959), pp. 110-113.

## 3. The Surprising God

Once Moses had recovered himself from the surprise of the burning bush, and the long memory of Abraham's God concerning the promise, Moses had presence of mind enough to ask a very significant question. Recall now, this question was addressed to El Shaddai, the Almighty God. It might seem an impertinence, were the question not so relevant. Moses put his question in the context of the predictable situation, assuming he dared to take this hope seriously: "If I come to the people of Israel and say to them, 'The God of your fathers has sent me to you,' and they shall ask me, 'What is his name?' what shall I say to them?" (Ex. 3:13, RSV). That, we have noted, was a very significant question.

Moses, of course, was a Hebrew in that moment. As Hebrew, he was asking for more than a casual introduction. He was asking to know just what God is like, the essential thrust of how God acts, so that a fellow could predict with a reasonable degree of certainty. For example, he wanted to know if this surprise of the burning bush that did not consume was characteristic of God. Was God capable of a continuing flow of improvisations? Or could he not really depend on God? The question was not dissimilar to our own: Can I really depend on God?

We recognize immediately (if we think about it at all) that Moses was not asking an academic question about God. He was asking about God in terms of human experience. In our way of speaking about it, Moses was asking: "Can I count on you?"

The translations of God's answer to Moses are almost endless in their variety—which may say something about the mystery of God. But any translation worth remembering must take into account the fact that *the only God we know* is the God of our own experience. We may speak of God in ways beyond our immediate knowing. But if God has any validity for us, that validity will be in terms of ourselves and our experience with him.

We may as well ask Moses' question for ourselves: How can I know I have brushed elbows with the Ancient of Days and learned that he can be counted on? Or can I? And the answer, it seems to me, will be in terms of our own experience. Let's attempt to answer our question by asking another: How can I know the truth of a mathematical axiom? (That is a question we ought to be able to handle.) Well, take the Pythagorean theorem: the sum of the squares of the two legs of a right triangle are equal to the square of the third side. Now, how can I know that? And the answer: by experience. All I need do is draw a right triangle on paper; measure the length of the two legs of the triangle; multiply each leg's length by itself; add the two products. Then, measure the other side of the triangle; multiply the length of that side by itself. And then compare the sum of the products with the product in the second procedure. They are equal. Ergo, I have experienced the truth of the mathematical axiom.

Now back to Moses' question and the answer given: What is your name? and the answer: "I, who have been with you always, will always be with you." That is not double-talk. Rather, God's answer to Moses' question was an invitation to Moses to do just what we did with the mathematical axiom: prove the truth by his own experience. In this case, Moses was invited to cast a backward glance over the way he had come to that moment: from the bulrushes, through the years in Pharaoh's palace; the ill-fated confrontation with the Egyptian slave master, the years in Midian, to this burning bush that did not consume. The invitation was to view the long pilgrimage of his life from a particular stance: the stance of faith. The invitation was to see Providence in the way he had come: "I who have been with you always . . ."

We may have difficulty seeing how God was in the way we have come. This may be particularly true if the way we

have come has been rough. Francis Thompson came over
such a way, and was blind to him who was with him in it:

> I fled Him, down the nights and down the days;
>   I fled Him, down the arches of the years;
> I fled Him, down the labyrinthine ways
>   Of my own mind; and in the midst of tears
> I hid from Him, and under running laughter.

But that is where God begins: with an invitation to recognize
that his presence has been with us, even when we were
blind to him, and could not or would not admit the reality.
The first half of God's answer to Moses' question, then, was
invitation: to admit the reality of his presence, always.

The second half of God's answer was promise: "I will
always be with you." What Moses desperately feared was
another failure. He trembled at the possibility of going down
to Egypt and falling flat on his face. He not only feared
failure; he feared for his life. He could not risk going way
out on a limb unless he could predict that God would be
with him. He needed reassurance. If the promise were simply
a benign, placid "presence," a kind of sentimental wishing
one well, he could do without it. The promise had to be
heavier than that. Otherwise he would be going without
much hope. And a man cannot go far without good hope.

So God was about to show Moses that the promise included a dynamic, innovative, creative use of improvisation
and surprise. He can take the old, familiar things and put
them together in a new way, so that the only way you
could describe the result would be with the word "miracle."
This God is not boxed in by rules men have discovered from
the world he, the Creator, made. There are patterns of
operation that only he knows. He can take the known and
the familiar, and the unknown and the unfamiliar, and put
them together in ways that no one ever dreamed of.

To demonstrate this surprising aspect of his power, God

asked Moses what it was he held in his hand. Now Moses thought it was a shepherd's rod. But when he threw it down at God's bidding, he discovered that it was a writhing serpent: something that had never entered his head. And the point is, for Moses and us: We have a God who is adequate. We can count on him. He may come in ways we had never thought of, and the help may be in a form we would never have anticipated, but the fact is: We can count on God. That is the basis for hope. And God's nature accounts for the surprising ways God uses to quicken hope.

Earlier I wrote that this way of understanding God rests on experience. Now may I share one of my own? I had served as pastor of the same congregation for more than twenty-one of my then twenty-eight years in the Christian ministry. Almost overnight, for reasons that were compelling and over which I had no real control, I thought it necessary to resign. The tensions of an uncertain future were better than the stress of a situation that could only deteriorate. Although faced with the collapse of my life work, and the severing of a long and most fulfilling relationship, I resigned.

Almost immediately, I was wrestling with the despair that may have been gnawing at Moses in Horeb. What hope does a man have when his life falls in around his ears? When threatened by loss and waste; when that to which he has given his life is suddenly gone; when all is stripped away: what does a man do then? First, he finds his own Horeb: a way to exist. And then he waits for God to work. Did someone care enough to ask the question: What are you going to do, he might well reply, "I'm going to wait for God's surprise."

In my own case, God worked in ways beyond my predicting. Our needs were more than supplied. My companion's professional status changed from graduate student to university professor overnight, and in a place much like Horeb—far removed from the scene of our brokenness. Work in my own profession opened. This book is a part of the door of opportunity God has given. I had feared that that which I held in my hand was a lifeless stick. But when I cast it aside, I discovered that it writhed with life. God broke in on my Horeb in surprise. And in that surprise, hope was revived.

That is the lesson, not only of my life, but the lesson of the Exodus, Bethlehem, and the empty tomb. God is capable of surprising us, and in that fact is another aspect of Christian hope.

# 5

## *Hope as Demand*

### Isaiah 33:20-24; Amos 5:18-24;
### Jeremiah 7:1-7; 26:1-24; 38:17-24

Mary Corita Kent has pointed out a surprising aspect of modern advertising. That aspect might be called the other-worldly overtones. On the surface, the advertisements praise the qualities of soft drinks, greeting cards, and automobiles. We are advised to "come alive"; to "care enough to send the very best"; to buy the brand automobile one "can really believe in." Miss Kent perceptively points out a common characteristic in these advertising catchwords: each has an appeal that goes beyond the product to a need in the user. In fact, the need may lie so deep as to be unrecognized—which makes the advertising the more potent. Who does not want to "come alive" with "the real thing"? To find something or someone he "can really believe in"? In our own setting, the spiritual and the secular are ambiguously joined.

But such union is not new. The men and women of Samaria in the eighth century B.C. had something they really believed in: "The day of the Lord." Starting out as a kind of idyllic vision of the future, the day of the Lord had become a favorite theme in the prophetic guilds of Israel. Like motherhood and pollution, the day of the Lord was a safe theme, and worthy, about 750 B.C.

Now, of course, this dream of the coming day of the Lord, and the lyric descriptions it called forth, were expressions of hope; hope that participated deeply in the religious life of the people of God. But Amos, that stern son of the desert, discerned a fatal flaw in this popularized version of hope, particularly, that brand of hope bandied about in the capital of northern Israel, Samaria. And he had some caustic comments for that hope, as recorded in his writings:

> Woe to you who desire the day of the Lord!.
> Why would you have the day of the Lord?
> It is darkness, and not light;
>     as if a man fled from a lion,
>     and a bear met him;
> or went into the house and leaned
>     with his hand against the wall,
>     and a serpent bit him.
> Is not the day of the Lord darkness,
>     and not light,
>     and gloom with no brightness in it?
>                                       (Amos 5:18-20, RSV)

The words strike with an almost physical impact. But is it that wrong to dream such a dream? to cherish such a vision? On the face of it, the oracle does not tell what lighted Amos' fire. You have to read between the lines to know what had drawn the prophetic comdemnation. And knowing helps. Put together, the picture adds up to something like this: The spiritual vision of the blameless day of perfect fulfilment had been totally secularized. Hope had been prostituted into the prediction of a Gross National Product that would put every Israelite on easy street. The God of hope had been exchanged for this particularized hope as god. All the hope demanded of its adherents was a kind of diabolical cleverness; an aptitude for making the system work to one's own advantage.

To such a distortion of hope, Amos lowered his plumb line: the day of the Lord would come, all right, but not as they had supposed. That "day" would be judgment day for

Samaria.

We cannot help but ask: How had hope gone so wrong? And why? For now, hold the questions in abeyance while we pursue the development of this hope in Judah. In earlier chapters we saw hope as promise, prompting the pilgrimage of Abraham; the saga of Jacob. In each instance, the hope was two-pronged: the seed and the land. Abraham never realized the promise of the land, having nothing more than a cave to call his own and that for his burial. Jacob, who had returned to the land from Paddan-aram in middle life, was driven by famine from the land, taking his seed and the promise into Egypt. The promise of land finally came up for redemption, beginning with Moses, continuing with Joshua, surviving the chaos of the period of the judges, being finally secured under David and Solomon. After the division of the land under Jeroboam I, especially bitter because of its fragmentation of the promised land, the little nation of Judah cherished and amplified the promise of the land. By the eighth century B.C. this promise had taken on universalistic dimensions. One of the popular oracles of that time, found in Micah and Isaiah, celebrated the hope that is in the promise. The words may be familiar:

> It shall come to pass in the latter days
>    that the mountain of the house of the Lord
> shall be established as the highest of the mountains,
>    and shall be raised above the hills;
> and all the nations shall flow to it,
>    and many peoples shall come, and say:
> "Come, let us go up to the mountain of the Lord,
>    to the house of the God of Jacob;
> that he may teach us his ways
>    and that we may walk in his paths."
>
> For out of Zion shall go forth the law,
>    and the word of the Lord from Jerusalem.

> He shall judge between the nations,
>   and shall decide for many peoples;
> and they shall beat their swords into plowshares,
>   and their spears into pruning hooks;
> nation shall not lift up sword against nation,
>     neither shall they learn war any more (Isa. 2:2-4,
>     RSV).

The vision popularized by this oracle came to a moment of truth in 701 B.C. when the Assyrian Sennacherib laid siege to Jerusalem. When the crisis passed, with a mysterious disaster befalling Assyria's besieging troops, King Hezekiah's faith was vindicated, and hope was enlarged. Isaiah, moved by their miraculous deliverance, celebrated Jerusalem's enlarged hope in an oracle that came to be a popular text for the next hundred years. The Isaianic oracle paints a tranquil, pacific scene:

> Look upon Zion, the city of our
>   appointed feasts!
> Your eyes will see Jerusalem,
>   a quiet habitation, an immovable tent,
> Whose stakes will never be plucked up,
>   nor will any of its cords be broken
>                               (Isa. 33:20, RSV).

But notice Isaiah's tense: "will be." This is the Jerusalem of the future; the Jerusalem of hope, celebrated in the here and now.

Imagination serves to depict some of the uses prophets may have made of that text when, a little more than one hundred years later, Jeremiah prophesied the desolation of Zion at the hand of Nebuchadnezzar of Babylon (Jer. 34:1-5). That they remembered the oracles of earlier prophets is attested in Jeremiah 26:16-19 when Micah of Moresheth is quoted at one of Jeremiah's trials. The popular idea of the

inviolability of Jerusalem because of the promise, made substantial in the Temple, had become the ground of a false
hope (Jer. 26:1-6). Poor, weak Zedekiah, whose lot it was
to preside over the collapse of the city and the kingdom,
must have leaned heavily on that hope when he read the
reports from the military after 588 B.C. But Jeremiah's doom-
saying came to pass; Isaiah's vision of hope was lost in the
dust and rubble of Zion's fall. Why had hope failed in
Judah?

In the answer to that question we have yet another shape
of hope: hope as demand. The demand was implicit in Isaiah's
vision. Perhaps he felt that the trauma of the Assyrian siege
would forever purge Judah of unfaithfulness. But if that
were his assumption, he was wrong: the children had to
learn for themselves the lessons of their fathers.

The provisional character of the promise (which is another way of speaking of the hope) can be seen more clearly
in Jeremiah's pronouncements. The earlier Temple sermon
of Jeremiah, which came about the year 608 B.C., was posi-
tively hopeful. However that hope was conditioned upon
their meeting the demand.

"For if you truly amend your ways and your doings, if you
truly execute justice with one another, if you do not oppress
the alien, the fatherless or the widow, or shed innocent blood
in this place, and if you do not go after other gods to your
own hurt, then I will let you dwell in this place, in the land
that I gave of old to your fathers for ever" (Jer. 7:5-7, RSV).
Later, when Judah continued her wilful ways, Jeremiah
engaged in one of his dramatic prophetic acts, involving the
Rechabites (Jer. 35). The point of the little drama was a
lesson in contrast: Whereas the Rechabites had met the
demand of their father, Judah had failed to meet the demand
of their promised hope. Therefore the hope was forfeit. (See
Jer. 35:12-17.)

From that point on, through the surrender in 597 B.C., and

the humiliation of Judah in the eleven-year vassalage of Zedekiah, the prophet became more and more explicit. (See Jer. 34:2-5; 36:27-31; 37:6-10; 38:17-23.) Hope for Judah lay beyond the Jerusalem they knew. They had forfeited the hope when they failed to meet hope's demand.

So much for the principle. But we are left with a question about our time: Does hope still levy its demand? And if so, what are hope's demands today? In answer, I would say: "Hope has her requirements still. First, hope demands that we look beyond her to her God. Second, hope asks that we shape our lives and our relationships so that she is not blocked in bringing her vision to pass." Another way of putting hope's demands (and yet saying the same thing) would be this: First, hope's proscription of idolatry; second, hope's prescription of morality. In each area, hope has her peculiar demands.

## 1. Hope and Idolatry

One of man's perennial temptations is to make hope's vision his god. You may recall that earlier in this chapter we asked what went wrong in Israel, that hope had been so distorted in the popular "day of the Lord" theme Amos decried. The answer to that question lies right here: Israel had taken hope's vision and made that their god. They had come to worship the bright, gaudy tinsel of their secularized version of hope. Their particularized hope was the thing desired, not God, who makes all hope possible. In Paul's classic analysis, "They exchanged the truth about God for a lie and worshiped and served the creature rather than the Creator" (Rom. 1:25, RSV). In other words, they were idolators.

Two manifestations of an idolatrous hope seem to be a part of our contemporary scene. One of these manifestations is found in our Western culture and effectively imposed upon Japan in the East as well: the idolatry of sacralized secularism. The other is found in the Communist ideology with its idolatry of the desacralized secularism. The former, like Jeremiah's Jerusalem in the time of the Temple of the Lord sermon, is less obvious in its idolatry than the latter. But the idolatry is present and is no less deadly. The evidence of this camouflaged idolatry is found in the quality of the lives and relationships the men who have that kind of hope build. Men in this persuasion skill sell their spiritual birthright for messes of pottage that go snap, crackle, and pop.

Karl Marx, the ideologist of modern communism, grew up in the tradition of the biblical hope. His father, a Jewish lawyer, became a Christian in 1824, and along with the members of his family, was baptized as a Protestant. Young Karl attended school at Treve, and after 1835, the universities at Bonn and Berlin, graduating with a Ph.D. in 1841. He had been fully exposed to the biblical traditions, including the promise and the hope.

But Marx turned away from all that. He said religion (and he was thinking particularly of the kind he knew best— the Christian religion) was an opiate; God an illusion; and if there was a god, their institutional religion an idolater. He made the indictment that churchmen had exchanged their eschatological birthright for a mess of secular pottage. He saw the church as having sold her vision of the future in the interest of a secure now.

How accurate is that indictment? One theologian of hope sees the kind of Christianity the church has fostered since the Reformation as inviting a radical rejection from those who see injustice now and wish for the church to take her place with others in striving to correct it. Perhaps a paragraph from his writings will make his position clear:

> For a long time faith in God has been saturated more with anxiety about the future than with hope in a new future of the earth. Time and again Christians have

searched in faith for the stability of eternity within the terrors of time. In the last century such a "faith without hope" elicited a "hope without faith." Because Christians believed in a "God without a future," those who willed the future of the earth had no option but to join forces with atheism and seek a "future without God." That is the schism of modern times from which many Christians and many atheists are suffering today. And if one views as heretics those atheists who seek a "future without God" in a hope without faith, then those believers who hold fast to a "God without future" in a faith without hope wear just as clearly the stripes of heresy. After messianic hopes wandered out of the church and were invested in progress, rebuilding, and revolutions, the church was left with only a half-truth. But should the knots of history be so tightly tied against the future? I think that this present dilemma can be overcome, but only if Christians call again upon the "God of hope" of the Old and New Testaments and testify to him practically and concretely in responsibility for the present.[1]

We may not agree with so radical a diagnosis. But we must ask how concerned Christians are to bring God's promised future into the here and now. Idolatry was the plague of God's people in the times of the prophets. Were Jeremiah to come upon the scene today, would he feel compelled to preach another Temple sermon?

In contrast to this sacralized idolatry of the outwardly religious West, the idolatry of communism is more obvious. Although the Communists have abandoned any faith in God, they do cling to their particular kind of hope. Titov, one of the first of the Russian spacemen, arrogantly confessed their

---

[1] Jurgen Moltmann, *Religion, Revolution and the Future* (New York: Charles Scribner's Sons, 1969), p. 20.

idolatrous creed in an off-hand comment about his experiences on his first space voyage:

> Some people say there is a God out there, but on my travels around the earth all day long I looked around and didn't see him. I saw no God or angels. Up to our first orbital flight by Yuri Gagarin no God helped build our rocket. The rocket was made by our people. I don't believe in God. I believe in man, his strength, his possibilities and his reason.[2]

Such brave confidence in man has yet to stand the test of time. The revelations of Stalin's excesses may have crumbled the toes of this new idol's foundations, but it is not yet toppled. True, some of the more perceptive have seen through this new god, but that fatal flaw has been effectively camouflaged, and the voices that have declared its flaw have been silenced. The idolatry, however, is there. Given time, the system will topple from its own inherent dissonance with the reality of man (as sinner) and history (as true to the character of a holy God).

## 2. Hope and Morality

The twin moral breaches against hope, and the God of hope, are presumption and desperation. Presumption assumes that the God who gave us our hope can be so shut up in our structures as to prevent his getting out, except by our sufferance.

We, of course, recognize this kind of presumption in others. The Roman Catholics, for example, with their strict Council of Trent interpretation of salvation through the church and by no other means, are an obvious example. What may not be quite so obvious is the quiet and proud assumption that our way is better, more productive, more effective in produc-

---

[2] *Knoxville News Sentinel,* May 7, 1962, Associated Press Report.

ing the true piety, than any other. By whatever form, this
kind of presumption can be detected by a certain careless-
ness in morality, either in the personal life or in the social
structures where such communions of hope predominate.
Isaiah the prophet, told a story in eighth-century Israel about
a vineyard, carefully planted, tended in hope, and advantaged
in every way (Isa. 5:1-6). But against every predictable
factor, the yield from that vineyard was disappointing; it
brought forth, according to the prophet, "stinking, wild
grapes." Then the prophet brought home the moral:

> For the vineyard of the Lord of hosts
>    is the house of Israel,
> and the men of Judah
>    are his pleasant planting;
> and he looked for justice,
>    but behold, bloodshed;
> for righteousness,
>    but behold, a cry! (Isa. 5:7, RSV).

Following the story is one of the most impassioned pleas
for social righteousness you will read anywhere (Isa. 5:8-
23). The lesson is clear: The people who have been given
hope are under demand. To fail to meet that demand is to
invite the judgment of God. Could that be the meaning for
us in the morass of our Southeast Asia involvement, and the
frightening sabre rattling of Communist China? Our God of
hope is a God who acts; his area is history; his actors are
the civilizations men build, under their leaders. The Chal-
deans were brutal, unjust, immoral. Yet, they were instru-
ments of God's judgment upon Judah and Israel, to the dis-
may of good men like Habakkuk and Zephaniah. The lesson
of salvation-history is: A people who have been given hope
must be pure. Presumption will lead to immorality, and the
forfeiture of hope's promise.

The other sin against hope, and the God of hope, is

desperation. If those who presume care too little, those who despair care too much. Desperation, when hope is lost, can take frightening forms. One is to become impatient to the point of indiscrimination. The urge to destroy, to burn, to kill is the mood of despair. Such wanton passion can be the cry of men and women who have lost hope, who have given over to despair. Such an one is told of by the journalist John Gerassi. She was a pregnant woman, living in the favelas, the hillside slums of Rio:

> "My first two babies died within a few months of their birth. Now I hope that this one will be a boy and that he will grow up to be strong so that he can avenge his dead brother and sister."
>
> I asked her who she thought was responsible. Her answer was blunt: "You!—and all the others like you who can afford those shoes and that suit.
>
> "I think just the money you paid for that pen could have saved one of my children."[3]

This kind of impatience with things as they are is the mark of one who has lost hope. The morality implied in hope is missing. The exploited will not wait for God, once they have come to despair. And in despair's wanton excesses is her sin against God, and the hope he has given and promised to bring to the light of man's day.

One final word, and we will bring to a close our theme of hope as demand. The church today is the true community of hope in our world. The question of vital import is this: Does our hope relate only to a point beyond history? Or does hope have something to do with history itself?

Perhaps the clue to answer those significant questions may be found in another question: How does God relate to his-

---

[3] From *The Great Fear in Latin America*, quoted by Steve Weissman, "New Left Man Meets the Dead God," Marty and Peerman, *New Theology No. 5* (The Macmillan Company, 1969), pp. 40-41.

tory? Does he relate only to a point beyond history? Or does God work in history itself?

The Bible, from beginning to end, is a book telling of God's mighty acts within the brackets of history—once we think about it. The Bible begins with a theological account of creation. As it begins, so this salvation history continues: God acting in history and through men in the call of Abram; in the Exodus under Moses; in the judgment of Israel's sins through defeat in war and captivity; in the restoration of Judah by the sufferance of the Persian, Cyrus. God's ultimate action in history to date, according to the Bible, is in the Christ event, by which God himself came into history: "God was in Christ reconciling the world unto himself" (2 Cor. 5:19). God's coming into history in the person of Jesus of Nazareth embraced the essentiality of the human condition, with this exception: the divine powers of being in Christ, once having submitted to death, overcame death by resurrection. That, too—according to the New Testament witness—occurred within history's framework. The book of Acts and the theme of Ephesians both emphasize the fact that God is continuing his work in the world through the church. And according to the New Testament, the blessed hope of Christ's return can be expected to come to fruition within history.

The lesson is clear: God acts within history. The province of God's concern (so far as the Bible informs us) is bounded by history. We were born within the brackets of history. In history God has met us in Christ. And in history God expects his people to meet hope's demands: a pure faith in him; morality in personal life; and the waging of continual war against the immorality and injustice which men tend to build into the structures of their society. Furthermore, by meeting hope's demands, we make credible our witness to the world of the hope that is in us.

# 6

## *Hope as Dimension*

### Romans 8:18-25

Imagine with me a lad who has never seen any photographic reproduction save a simple photograph. All objects of the photograph are in one plane. Perception of depth, if any, is in terms of perspective. His mind may supply the lost dimension of depth, but all that meets his eye is the simple one-plane dimension.

Then one day, he is introduced to the stereopticon. Following instructions, he puts the device to his eyes, makes the necessary adjustments, and is confronted by a whole new dimension of reality. Added to his experience with photography is depth. The stereopticon has added depth to the plane.

Now bring to his accumulating experiences a viewing of Cinerama, the motion-picture projection system that took the stereopticon principles and added motion; the illusion of movement to the perception of depth. The new experience is the nearest yet to real life. In fact, as the roller coaster tops the incline, beginning its downward plunge, he finds himself gripping the armrests of his theater seat to hold on— so real is the sensation.

When one stops to analyze the dimensions of perception our lad has passed through, we see that from the flat plane he proceeded to the perception of depth. Finally, to these was added the simulated sensation of motion. Now these are spatial dimensions, of course, but they can serve as an analogy for the dimensions of Christian hope. Hope takes on biblical shape when it incorporates the time dimensions of the present, the past, and the future. Though not explicitly stated in that way, the apostle Paul seems to have had such in mind in Romans 8:24-25: "For in this hope we were saved. Now hope that is seen is not hope. For who hopes for what he sees? But if we hope for what we do not see, we wait for it with patience" (RSV). On the face of it, the apostle is writing from the stance of the here and now. It is in this "present," according to Paul, that we hope. But hope has the characteristic of the "not yet"; hope remains unseen. That is, hope vitalizes the present, but remains beyond it. So, almost explicitly, we have in Paul's word on hope the time dimensions of the present and the future. But what of the past? We shall see, in due course, that the past participates in the present and the future in very vital ways, and is implicit in all that the apostle says. We have then in hope these time dimensions: present, past, and future.

## 1. Hope's Present

The generation under thirty has informed us of something we had almost forgotten: the present as a real dimension of life. Urging their peer group to live in the "now," they emphasize the reality of the present. And a grain of truth in their stance smarts us. Our goal-oriented approach to living has the very real result of sacrificing the present in favor of the future. Awareness in the "now" is a needed note. One of the by-products of our long-range, deferred-gratification kind of living has been the tendency to think we will really begin to live sometime out in the future. But this goal-oriented approach to living has the built-in flaw of desensitizing us to living in the present. Like children, we wish our lives away. We think we will be really living, once we acquire that new car, or that degree, or that new home, or that job promotion, or that baby—or whatever. We can exchange the birthright of the present for any one of many messes of future pottage.

Perhaps we should pay attention to the existentialists who taught that we must reverence the "now" as the only time we have. Nor can we ignore the significance of the fact that the first to draw attention to the here and now as the only temporal reality was a Christian: that dour Dane, Kierkegaard. But Kierkegaard's truth was ignored by Christians generally, and adopted by the philosophers in a desacralized sense: the existentialists. Perhaps the distortion of the "now" people of our day can be understood, partially at least, in the Christian's failure to see the needed corrective in the Dane's truth, while the atheists Camus, Sartre, and others saw it and taught the authentic life lived out in terms of the present.

But what the existentialists saw, and Christians generally missed, was truly Christian. For evidence, we need only to turn to Luke's inaugural frontispiece, in which Jesus' announcement of his messianic mission was set forth in terms of setting wrongs right: "To preach good news to the poor . . . to proclaim release to the captives and recovering of sight to the blind, to set at liberty those who are oppressed, to proclaim the acceptable year of the Lord" (5:18-19, RSV).

This was a radical vision; surely too radical for that "present" as we read later on. But the immediacy of Jesus' vision was described by our Lord in terms of the present: "Today this scripture has been fulfilled in your hearing." (See Luke 4:21, RSV.)

The charge has been made that Christians have defused the urgent immediacy of Christ's mission because of its radicalism. However, Christ insisted on that very radicalism as having come into their "now." Our "now"—like that of Jesus' contemporaries—cannot seem to bear such dissonance; we have extracted his radical discontent from our understanding of his gospel, disclaiming any mandate upon us to share his sense of urgent immediacy. If one researcher can

be believed, we have been fairly successful as followers of
the Christ in divorcing any social concern from Christian
discipleship:

> Many research studies have shown that there are sig-
> nificant differences in beliefs and attitudes between
> Jews, Catholics, and Protestants, and even between
> various Protestant denominations. Most disturbing are
> findings that show that the religious devout are on the
> average more bigoted, more authoritarian, more dog-
> matic, and more antihumanitarian than the less devout.
> Such findings are disturbing from a religious standpoint
> because they point to a social institution that needs to
> be reformed. They are disturbing from an antireligious
> standpoint because they point to a social institution that
> deserves to be destroyed.[1]

But Christ was content with nothing less than a radical
"now" in the time dimension of the present. We may have
played, by our timidity about the possibilities inherent in
our "now," into the hands of our antagonists. When the present is almost too much to bear, history teaches that one of
two things likely will happen. The deprived may strike out
against the institutions of the vested interests of their time,
seeking to destroy that which oppresses. (Recall the American, French, and Russian revolutions?) Or the deprived may
forget the "now" in a celebration of "what will be." So one
of my Negro minister friends, speaking out of the frustration
of his life situation, could only complain: "My folks don't
count themselves as having been to church unless I put on
the 'rousements for them. I got to fascinate them with how
good it's gonna be so they can forget how bad it is now."

Preoccupation with what will be may have satisfied pre-
vious generations of his kind, but not now. They know that

---

[1] Milton Rokeach, "Peace, Hope, Bigotry," *Psychology Today*, April,
1970, p. 33.

hope has something to do with the "now" as well as the future. When one lives in hope, he cannot be content with things as they are in the here and now. Not if he has Christ's kind of hope. For hope's dimension in the "now" is discontent; discontent with anything that is dissonant with God's good intention.

## 2. The Past

Earlier we mentioned the "now" people, taking their cue from such existentialists as Camus and Sartre, but distorting their emphasis on authentic living to mean nothing more than sensual indulgence. Living came to be a heightened awareness of sensation, of relatedness, of life now. A part of a whole generation lived out their youthful years under the idea that life is nothing more than the "now." They had a slogan: "Make love not war"; and a theme: "flower power." They celebrated hope's vision in sensual now.

The disconcerting aspect of those flower children's motto was that they had a grain of truth in it. Their vision of what life ought to be reflected a kind of prophetic dream of the future. But their truth was held in isolation, and that always leads to distortion. They misunderstood the meaning of the word "love," so glibly inscribed on their slogan. The double entendre was taken in its basest sense. Hope's vision, uninformed by the moral lessons of the past, soon descended to nothing more than a biological act. The flower children did make love in their now. Uninformed by the past of the moral consequences of such unstructured relationships, they spawned a second generation of little flower children who wander the streets of Haight-Asbury and Greenwich Village— unloved, uncared for, bodies and minds bearing the marks of their misguided parents. What went so wrong? The past has many lessons by which to inform hope, one of which is: "The sins of the fathers are visited on their children, unto the third and fourth generations." The original flower children, who sought to live in the now, who sought to seize hope's vision and draw it into their present, who sought to live in heightened awareness and tender relatedness, had not bothered to learn the moral lessons of the past. Hence, the issue of their skewed hope came into the world marked by disrupted genetic links, unstructured home and family situations, and no future.

The lesson drawn from this citation of the contemporary scene is this: the past is not unrelated to hope. The past informs hope, not only of moral truth, but of the ways in which her God has stretched forth his hand to help and to save. That particular interpretation of history in the eastern rim of the Mediterranean from the fifteen century B.C. to the first century A.D. is called "salvation-history," a way of saying that the Bible reads its history theologically. In the events of men's lives and nations the holy men of old saw the mighty hand of God. So the writer of Psalm 78, recalling bits of the salvation-history of his people (vv. 42-55), marvels that they have so soon forgotten. But hope does not forget: what God has done, God will do. Hope is informed by the past of her gracious God.

Moreover, the past gives to hope a certain inspiration. Hope faces the discouraging aspect of the present, the "what is," and admitting its harsh reality, is tempted to give up. But then, hope remembers what God has done: the exodus, the restoration from captivity, the resurrection, Pentecost. Discouraged hope, inspired by analogous events out of the past, dares to hope again.

And in the process, the past gives to hope the language, the symbols, by which she can express herself. The exodus becomes every man's deliverance from bondage. The Jordan becomes every man's boundary between the harsh present and the future promise. The promised land becomes hope's destiny. The resurrection becomes hope's promise to every man who will receive God's Christ. Hope, which looks to the future, has her roots in the past.

### 3. The Future

But hope, oriented toward the future, lives in the present. Yet in the present, hope has the characteristic of creating dissonance. That is, hope sees the possibilities inherent in the present: things could be better than they are. Hope, by its very nature, is disjunctive with the present, seeking always to make the present more like its vision of the future. Hope is in the present as challenge, as judgment, as promise.

And the church, which is the community of hope, takes on this aspect when she is truly church. By her very life she is a demonstration of the new humanity, living in the present, but looking toward the new Jerusalem, the new heaven and the new earth. As a matter of fact, the idea of the possible that is "not yet" but can be, runs all the way through the Bible. Jeremiah spoke of the *new* covenant (Jer. 31). Joel wrote of a *new* time when God's sons and daughters would be under the compulsion of hope's reality, dreaming dreams and seeing visions so real they could not but strive to make the new real (Joel 2:28-29). Rightly, the apostles saw Pentecost as the dawning of Joel's day of hope (Acts 2:17-21), and explained their new spirit of toughness as the gift of the Spirit. Jesus spoke of the *new* testament in his blood (1 Cor. 11:25). John had a vision of a *new* earth and a *new* Jerusalem (Rev. 21:1-2). All the way through the new—the future—is breaking in on the old—the present. And the consummation of this new reality is the church, divinely intended to embody this newness in the now (Eph. 4-5).

If the church is true to her vocation in the world, she will be disjunctive. That is, she will stand out from her surroundings as different, as new, as better. Perhaps we can see the disjunctive aspect of the church—the community of hope bringing the future into the now—better concretely. In 1967

I visited East Berlin, the vital center of European communism. Much of what we saw was depressing: the war-ravaged public buildings, standing as mute evidence of the carnage and senseless brutality war spawns; the barren uniformity of dress and manner; the almost pathetic pride in their public works, erected since the Communists took over. And then our guide swung the bus into something new: a wide boulevard. Flowers, shrubs, and trees between sparkling fountains made the grassy center mall a new Eden. Lovely modern shops and office buildings lined the broad and inviting walks beyond. This was new; the contrast with all that we had seen was inescapable. Did this street belong here in East Berlin? And then our guide explained: This was Karl Marx Allee, the street of the future set down in the now. This was the street of tomorrow. Here in the now was what tomorrow would be like.

God has given the world Christ's church. Her business is to be disjunctive: to exist as the new humanity in the midst of the old. One of her functions in this disjunctive stance is judgment. The other is promise. God's church is the promise of his intention.

Martin Marty, in the Cole lectures at Vanderbilt University Divinity School in 1970, told of visiting the Oberlin College campus in Ohio. On that campus, among the old Ivy League traditional buildings, is the new, radically different Yamasaki Building. At one point, Dr. Marty overheard two alumni attempting to adjust to the disjunctive aspect of the new, alongside the old. "How do you like the new building?" one asked the other. "All right. But it doesn't fit the environment," came the answer. "It will. It will," was the reply. Dr. Marty went on to comment that he did not hear any more and could not tell the meaning of that remark. But we can see a meaning in it.

Whenever God's future confronts our now, the result is disjunctive. It doesn't fit the environment. But hope speaks to the present out of God's future and replies, "It will, It will." Wasn't that what the Johannine writer meant when he wrote: "The darkness is passing away and the true light is already shining" (1 John 2:8, RSV). Hope, informed by the past, living in the present, draws the future into the now by the power of Christ's Spirit, demonstrating to the world the divine intention and what—under God—will be.

# 7

## *Hope as Resurrection*

### 1 Corinthians 15:12-22

The early nineteenth-century French statesman-bishop Talleyrand was, on an occasion, in conversation with a certain M. Lepeaux. Lepeaux was confiding his disappointment in the meager success his attempt to establish a new religious movement had met. Lepeaux regarded his innovation as an improvement on Christianity. He explained that, in spite of all the efforts he and his followers had put forth, they were advanced very little in their efforts to gain adherents. He asked for advice as to what to do.

Talleyrand replied that it was indeed difficult to found a new religion, more difficult, indeed, than one would imagine at the beginning of such an enterprise; so difficult he scarcely knew what to advise. "Still," he said—after a moment's reflection—"there is one plan you might at least try. I should recommend you to be crucified and to rise again on the third day."

Note the interesting fact that Talleyrand did not stop with a suggestion of martyrdom. Giving one's life for a way of understanding truth is not new to the human race. In that brave company are many of the noblest of the human race: Socrates, most of the apostles, John Huss, Servetus, George Wishart, Thomas Cranmer, Bishop Ridley, William Wallace, and—you name your favorites!

A poet draws a very large circle:

A picket frozen on duty—
    A mother starved for her brood—
Socrates drinking the hemlock,
    And Jesus on the rood;
And millions who, humble and nameless,
    The straight, hard pathway trod—
Some call it Consecration,
    And others call it God.

We may not agree that Jesus belongs in the same breath with these others, but the point here is: many have given their lives for that which they believed in deeply. But Talleyrand's advice to Lepeaux did not stop with crucifixion; it went on to include resurrection. And that, obviously, is a new thing. So new, in fact, that it can be included as one of the biblical shapes of hope. But more, we shall see that without the resurrection of Jesus, hope from the Bible would have little substantial shape at all.

The question is sometimes raised: Was the resurrection of Jesus as recorded in the New Testament the creation of faith? Or was the resurrection of Jesus as found in the New Testament the creator of the faith we find reflected there? Above we made the point that others have died for the truth they held and that held them. If all we have in Jesus is his noble death, and the resurrection is only the illusion of pious minds, then one must ask: Why did not Socrates' followers "create" a resurrection for him? To ask the question is to make the whole idea collapse of its own weight.

What of the alternative: that the resurrection created faith? The keystone in the disciples' arch of faith was the fact of the resurrection. When one reads the New Testament accounts, he is struck all over again by the transformation the resurrection made in the disciples. That which had been held as a tentative conclusion (recall the denial of Peter; the scattering of the twelve) became a fixed conviction—after the resurrection. Thomas, who was the last to surrender, came under the power of the resurrected Christ at a private meal. His response, like all the others, was to cry out, "My Lord, and my God!" This cry was the summary of that faith grown sure by the resurrection.

Al Capp, creator of Li'l Abner and Daisy Mae, has created a technique for the entertainment of large audiences. Using a projection machine that carries his sketching to a screen fifty feet away, Mr. Capp draws each character of his famous comic strip so that the identity of each is obscure. Then, having gotten audience response as to the possible identity of each, Mr. Capp adds the last bold line, and says: "This is the line that makes the difference." With that line added, the audience knows the character.

The resurrection was the "line that made the difference." The event strengthened faith where faith had wavered; it created faith where faith had been wanting (as with James). For crucifixion—the giving of one's life for what one believes —is what men can do. Resurrection is what God can do. Crucifixion is an admission of weakness. Resurrection is a declaration of power. Crucifixion is the shape of a final challenge. Resurrection is the shape of an invincible hope.

In these next pages we shall seek to explore hope as refracted through the resurrection of Jesus. We shall make our exploration under the captions of declaration, definition, and dynamic.

## 1. Resurrection as Declaration

When Jesus came preaching in Galilee, his preaching was cast in the mold of an announcement; a declaration of realization. Carl Braaten has a few descriptive sentences that will help this fact come clear:

> Jesus did not go before his hearers with the information that there is such a thing as the kingdom of God;

that would have been no news to them. What he an-
nounced was that the kingdom was drawing so near
that its impact was already being impressed through
him. The eschatological day is dawning; its glimmerings
are already breaking out in Jesus' works and words.[1]

We saw that this declaration had the impact of the future
upon the now. It came into Nazareth as the radical demand
of God, judging anything dissonant with God's intention. The
demand was not impersonal; it was personal. Jesus said, "This
day is this scripture fulfilled in your ears" (Luke 4:21), and
his hearers understood.

For the Day of the Lord had been declared by the Old
Testament prophets. We saw earlier how this prophetic declaration was secularized; indeed, idolatrized. That is, they
worshiped their gaudy, tinselized version of the Day of the
Lord, while turning from God who was the source of the
hope it represented. In so doing, they missed the supra-
historical character of the Day. God's Day, as painted by the
prophets, transcended all the contradictions man has passed
upon himself and his kind. For God's Day participated not
at all in the usual characteristics of history. That is, the Day
of the Lord was defined as a day when men's relationships
would be without conflict, injustice, or exploitation. It would
be a Day when men worshiped God freely, and without any
taint of self-interest. The Day of the Lord would be a day
when beasts, men, and nations would lay aside all natural
antipathies and dwell together in peace. (See Isa. 2:2-4;
Mic. 4:1-4.) In plain words, the Day of the Lord was a
reality that lay beyond the intact world as we know it. The
Day of the Lord was a declaration of the divine intention
beyond history.

---

[1] Carl E. Braaten, *The Future of God* (New York: Harper & Row,
Publishers, 1969) p. 71. Reprinted by permission of Harper & Row,
Publishers, Inc.

And that intention, Jesus declared at Nazareth and else-
where, was now realized by his presence. We can understand,
then, why influential religious leaders gagged at Jesus' declaration. When one reflects upon it a bit, the impact hits
hard: Jesus' declaration was more than an announcement of
a development. It was a claim about himself. He, himself,
was supra-historical! He was, himself, from beyond the
brackets of time. Though participating in the process of
history at that very time, he was not history's child. Not
completely. He was God's self-disclosure. He was, in the
form of human personality, the divine intention spelled out.
The *eschaton* had invaded time. The Day of the Lord was
now being realized.

Seen in this light, the opposition to Jesus becomes more
understandable. That opposition came from the evil that was
in men, and that is over men. The crucifixion was predictable.
In a war to the death, each side exhausts its powers. Death
was evil's final power.

Now, had Jesus been nothing more than a demented man
—however noble in intention—his life and ministry would
have been nothing more than another tragic chapter in mankind's history. But Jesus had powers of being that were of
God. So when, and we say this reverently, evil had played
its trump card—death—God played his hand out. In God's
hand was resurrection. That meant the death of death. By
the resurrection the divine intention was reasserted. The
resurrection was God's dramatic declaration, which Braaten
has summed as follows:

> The resurrection was an act by which God identified
> himself with the cause of Jesus, vindicating Jesus' claim
> to represent the future of God in his earthly ministry.
> At the same time, the resurrection was an act of God by
> which the cause of Jesus could be continued in history,
> as an ongoing promise in the life of mankind for a future

share in the new reality which occurred already in the Messiah Jesus. The resurrection was thus the pivotal point by which God defined himself retroactively in the life of Jesus.[2]

The resurrection was a declaration of intent: God will have the last word. Man, nor the powers of evil, can thwart God in that.

Implicit in this declaration—and you have already noted it, doubtless—is the fact of divine power. God can make such a final declaration because he has the power to do so. But what is the motivation behind that power? Is it to reclaim a lost kingdom? to defeat man's enemy, put down insurrection, and restore man and history to its rightful sovereign?

Now though such a confrontation of powers is one way of understanding God's action, it does raise a serious question about the character of God: Is God, after all, concerned for "saving face"? Surely God's concern runs deeper than that. Such a construction of the divine intention rises to no greater height than a base, cosmic showdown. Perhaps the clue we seek for understanding can be found in those three simple, but magnificently profound, words: "God is love" (1 John 4:16). God's object was not that of a king seeking a lost kingdom, but of a lover seeking a lost love. His power was made to serve his love. God's declaration in Jesus' life, ministry, death, and resurrection was that of a lover.

## 2. Resurrection as Definition

As definition, the resurrection of Jesus is personal in its implication, a fact that was affirmed by John in his letter: "Beloved, we are God's children now; it does not yet appear what we shall be, but we know that when he appears we shall be like him, for we shall see him as he is" (1 John

---

[2] *Ibid.*, p. 73.

3:2, RSV). The phrase "as he is" lies, admittedly, beyond the limits of our present understanding. In writing to the Corinthians, the apostle Paul fell back upon a series of analogies when attempting to give shape to the idea of resurrection. Were we to put the gist of his arguments in plain English, that statement would be something like this: There are different orders of creation. This life is one order; the resurrection is of another. The attempt to read from one to the other is futile, if one seeks to read in fine detail. They have some commonality, but they have more that is not common. The differences are more significant than the likenesses. And then the analogies are ticked off: the planted seed and the grown plant; the different kinds of flesh: of the fish, the beast, the bird; the radiance of the sun, the moon, the stars (1 Cor. 15:35-50). The point of these analogies is that the resurrection is a new thing under the sun.

The resurrection of Jesus is, in several respects, explicit in its definition of this new thing. First, the resurrection was of one individual, Jesus, by himself. That, in contrast to the belief, held by the Jews of that day, of the mass resurrection of all mankind, helps define the characteristics of resurrection. The resurrection life was the gift of God to the *person;* the person who received that life through faith in God's Christ. Then, the resurrection occurred within history; it did not end history. The message of that fact was that in Jesus' resurrection a model of last things had come, particularly as they related to the believer. Moreover, that portent had come in the believer's here and now, which meant that the power of the resurrection life could be experienced partially within this life (Heb. 10:20-21). And, that which occurred in history (the resurrection of Jesus), but belonged beyond history, pointed to the believer's final salvation that was yet to come (1 Pet. 1:3-9). A final definition in the explicit historical fact of Jesus' resurrection was that in the resurrection a new mode of being had been given. The resurrection life was a new thing.

Emphasis must be given to the radical newness of Jesus' resurrection as a new mode of being. Continuity there was, sufficient for recognition by his friends. But discontinuity there was, too. The resurrection body of Jesus was not subject to time-space-place-movement limitations. This was, and is, existence of a new order. Revivification, or restitution to Adam's innocence and natural immortality, are not sufficient to exhaust the meaning of the resurrection. Here is life that has gone forward to a new condition; an exodus on the far side of death's domain, and a union with God in the fulness of glory.

In these ways, the resurrection of Jesus is explicit. Yet, the veil of mystery remains. When the apostle Paul sought to comfort and reassure shaken and grieving Christians at Thessalonica, he would not tolerate a breathless curiosity about details (1 Thess. 4:14-17). Rather, he was restrained, as Charles Erdman pointed out:

> The reserve and the restraint of′ the apostle are re-
> markable. He speaks in figures which he does not in-
> terpret, nor does he let his imagination play upon details
> which must have been alluring. He sums up the whole
> message of blessedness and glory, not by descriptions of
> physical or material splendor, but in one great spiritual
> reality: "So shall we ever be with the Lord."[3]

As definition, the resurrection of Jesus is also cosmic in implication. Here is the archstone of that "newness" about which the Old Testament prophets wrote. You will recall the salient features: men relating to men in trust, openness, and love; men worshiping God in spontaneous desire and fulness of joy; nations waging peace instead of war; the

---

[3] Charles R. Erdman, *The Epistles of Paul to the Thessalonians* (Philadelphia: The Westminster Press, 1935) p. 58.

antipathies of man and nature's creatures put aside. But how is such a dream achieved? We have already said that the dream was supra-historical. Is there no place for progress? Or does all wait upon some supra-historical intervention? Say, something like Christ's second coming?

A part of the answer lies in the fact that the men who have experienced God's caring love in Christ participate in the historical process. They are to go forth into the world in that same caring love they have experienced in Christ. This is a way of describing the community of hope, the church. The church is the community of caring persons, demonstrating to jaded men the divine intention. In that sense, as we have seen, the church is the community of the future in the here and now.

But history itself goes on, the larger stream absorbing and being influenced by the stream flowing within it. Modification, however, not transformation, is the effect. Nor is the redemption—actual redemption—being observably accomplished, either of history or of the cosmos. Indeed, that which was, is. And perhaps worse than that. Indeed, according to the ecologists, man by his sin has pushed the cosmos ever closer to a final disaster. The question can be put in the prophetic metaphor: Will the lion ever lie down with the lamb?

The resurrection of Jesus is clue, if not definition, pointing toward our answer. If the whole created order groans in travail under the bondage to sin and death even until now, then all awaits that which we find in the resurrection: redemption. Man may make small steps toward realization of that which is represented by the Day of the Lord. But man, history, and the cosmos await with breathless anticipation God's own coming: the second coming and final judgment. The resurrection of Jesus is promise of that. And without that, there is no real hope.

## 3. Resurrection as Dynamic

Does the resurrection hope make any real difference to modern man; the man who has "come of age" in a technological society? Resurrection made a difference in the days when the church was young, that we know. But what of now?

Let death become personal, in the stead of academic, and the old enemy is recognized for what he is: the enemy. In a moving account of her father's death, Svetlana Alliluyeva tells of the moment when the authorities came to take her father's body away. As you live through that moment with her, see if you identify:

> Late that night—rather, when it was near daybreak—they came to take the body for the autopsy. I started shaking all over with a nervous tremble. The body was laid on a stretcher . . . It was a beautiful body. It didn't look old or as if it had been sick at all. With a pang like a thrust of a knife in the heart, I felt what it meant to be "flesh of the flesh." I realized that the body that had given me life no longer had life in it, yet I would go on living.[4]

Death, even in a society that declares God beyond belief, is capable of striking the "knife in the heart." Death, no matter what the society or culture, has the capacity to drive man to the ultimate question: Is that all there is?

Some have sought to translate individual concern about ongoing life into social process. But the promise of a better society in the future is no real fulfilment to the individual, so long as the individual remains more than social process. Some have declared man's concern for ongoing life as "extra-territorial," not open to verifiable answers. Still others have

---

[4] *Life*, September 15, 1967, p. 106. Excerpt from *Twenty Letters to a Friend*, copyright Harper & Row, Publishers, Inc., 1967; reprinted by permission of Harper & Row, Publishers, Inc.

posited, from observation, or by analogy, or through intimation, such answers as transmigration, natural immortality,
and reincarnation. In essence those views seek to explain
death in terms of life's outer shell. But death is more than
that, as Braaten poignantly affirms: ". . . Death wants and
gets more than the outer shell. It penetrates to the inner
core of existence, cracks it open, and takes all there is to
take."[5]

The resurrection of Jesus is the Christian answer to death.
That answer is declaration, definition, and dynamic. Braaten
continues his paragraph, and says it well enough for both of
us: "The solution . . . to the problem of death is not to try
to negotiate a settlement, hoping that the enemy will be
decent enough to acknowledge the infinite value of some
immortal part that is 'extraterritorial,' beyond its jurisdiction.
The only extraterritoriality that Christian hope knows is the
life of the resurrected Christ who brings victory through and
beyond death."[6]

Talleyrand was right. Resurrection is fundamental. Christianity would be nothing without the resurrection of Jesus.
But with that resurrection we have another shape of biblical
hope.

---

[5] Braaten, *op. cit.*, p. 80.
[6] *Ibid.*, p. 80.

# 8

## *Hope as Expectation*

### 1 Peter 1:3-5; 1 John 3:3

What happens to a person when hope flickers, and threatens to flame out? As good an answer to that question as you will find comes from the pen of a modern writer, who is in tune with the tenor of our times—on the visceral level:

> Men . . . can fight back against big things. What kills them is erosion; they get nudged into failure. They get slowly scared. I'm scared. Long Island Lighting Company might turn off the lights. My wife needs clothes. My children . . . shoes, and fun, and . . . education. And the monthly bills and the doctor and teeth and a tonsillectomy . . . and suppose I get sick? Course you don't understand. It rots your guts away. I can't think beyond next month's payment on the refrigerator. I hate my job and I'm scared I'll lose it.[1]

Not only is nerve gone in such a man, but so is hope. And any expectation remaining in such a frame of reference is tinged with doom.

We would expect such morose pessimism from the worldling. No wonder, since he is without any underpinnings for his life, he is awash on the tide of economic necessities, family emergencies, and work insecurities. He has no sure anchor for his life, and this inner shriveling is predictable. What is not so predictable is that the man of faith should

---

[1] John Steinbeck, *The Winter of Our Discontent* (New York: Viking Press, 1961), p. 13.

also have the willies. To lose the note of joy and high expectation is not expected of the Christian. But bandied about
by such practical concerns as a rising economic demand from
family, competition on job or in profession (with a push from
the bottom side and a squeeze on the top side), the technologies explosion, obsolescence, shifts in public tastes, vari-
ance of acceptability in competence or performance, many
a Christian has fallen into the habit of running scared.

Nor is this a new thing under the sun. In *Pages from an
Oxford Diary*, Paul Elmer More writes of Oxford, that magnificent center of learning and piety created by the church.
The ironic contradiction between the ancient churches,
chapels, and buildings, erected as mute memorials of an
ancient faith, and the God-forsakenness in the faces of his
contemporaries, he contrasts in this way:

> Often I ask myself how it can be that dead stones and
> mortar should speak more eloquently of the divine
> presence than does the living face of man, made in the
> likeness of his Creator . . . I meet them and scrutinize
> their faces with insatiable curiosity. If many of them
> have found God or know his peace, it is a secret not re-
> vealed to me.

He writes of Newman, and of his presence haunting the place.
He tells of looking at pictures taken in youth, maturity, and
in old age. And then he sums up his impressions:

> And this is what I see. Instead of growing in grace
> and strength and peace, his features show what I can
> only call a steady deterioration. The end is almost ter-
> rible, so plainly written on the old man's countenance
> are the marks of anxiety and strain and a kind of pathetic
> fear . . . possibly it was that he beheld God, yet missed
> the peace of heaven.[2]

---

[2] As quoted in *Pulpit Digest,* June, 1965, pp. 11-12.

Now if the state of expectation is so low among men whose lives and living are secured by appointment and stipend from a state church, what of the man of the cloth whose tenure is subject to any church business meeting, and whom all the honored indicators seem to indict as incompetent and ineffective? And what of the layman, whose opportunity to clasp the horns of the altar are more remote?

Expectation is a part of the current scene, to be sure. But with many, it is not the expectation of hope. To such a doleful mood, hope has something to say. Perhaps that message can be summarized by three words: vitality, variety, and creativity. About these three words, and their encouragement to our hope, we concern ourselves here.

### 1. Vitality and Hope

The word vitality comes from the Latin word *vitae*, meaning life. Not for naught do we say, "Where there is life there is hope." In fact, the converse may also be confidently expressed: "Where there is no hope, there is no life." Or, at least, not for long. Physical life, a kind of dispirited existence, may go on. But the vitality will have been wrung out. Why is that so?

In answer, I would say that vitality is lost to life when the expectation of something good about to happen is lost. Lose that expectation, and one loses vitality: the power to sustain frustration—which power is the gift of hope. On the lowest level, let me cite for you an experiment with a chimpanzee named Sultan, conducted by the eminent psychologist Kohler. Just beyond Sultan's reach in his cage was fruit—fruit that Sultan liked very much. Moreover, Sultan was hungry. And to Sultan were given two bamboo sticks, one smaller than the other, so that one fit into the other, making a longer stick. Sultan immediately sought to reach the fruit with one stick or the other, or using each stick in tandem with the other; but his efforts met with failure. Sultan finally gave up, turned his back on the fruit, and sat down on his box on the far side of his cage. In a few minutes, however, he picked up the sticks and began playing with them. By chance, he poked the smaller stick into the larger. Immediately he perceived that his problem was solved. With his new tool, he ran to the side of the cage nearest the fruit, and with great animation and delight, began to pull in the fruit, not even taking time to eat it.[3]

Kohler pointed out that before discovering the sticks could be joined, Sultan was listless, apathetic—the picture of despair. After the discovery, Sultan was vital, active—the epitome of confidence. And it dawns on us that the difference, even on this lowest level of behavior, is that between hopelessness and hopefulness. When one has hope, one has life.

The behavioral psychologists, without intending to encourage any philosophical or theological conclusions on man's origins, have taken the behavior of an animal like Sultan as a means of understanding the dynamics of human behavior. Taking their method as a clue, recall with me the apostles after the crucifixion. Can you think of a more forlorn group? One had committed suicide; one had openly denied knowing Jesus; they were huddled together behind closed doors. Why? They had no hope! And without hope, no vitality.

In contrast, remember the apostles at Pentecost, after having been convinced that God had given them the means in Christ to meet and master death and the grave. A bolder, more self-assured crowd you will never find. What had happened? They had been given hope. And with hope, vitality. That is the nature of life. Once life is animated through the discovery of resurrection hope, the vitality given must be expressed in action. The flurry of the disciples' action in the days beyond Pentecost was, phychologically under-

[3] O. Hobart Mowrer, *Learning Theory and the Symbolic Process* (New York: John Wiley & Sons, Inc., 1960), pp. 230-36.

stood, the flower of their revived hope. Speaking of that action theologically, the apostles were energized by the hope mediated to them through Christ's abiding and indwelling Spirit.

At least one other aspect of hope's vitality must be noted, in addition to the energizing effect hope gives. That other aspect of hope is courage. Hope has the effect of mediating courage. The behavioral psychologists, again, can help us understand, from a dynamic point of view, how hope gives the gift of courage. We are moved to act from the motive of expectation, rather than the anguish of fear.

In Pavlov's famous experiments on conditioned reflexes with his dogs, one experiment involved presenting food to hungry dogs after they had been exposed to a slight electrical shock. The dogs came to anticipate the food, and in the course of the experiment (although the level of electric shock was raised to the pain threshold) the dogs—in expectation of food—manifested only the conditioned reflexes anticipatory to receiving food. By the experiment, the anticipation of pleasure blocked the fear that the pain stimulus would have otherwise induced.

Commenting on that emotional transformation, Mowrer relates an incident reported by Frolov in *Pavlov and His School:* The story is told by the scientist G. Bohn, that when Sherrington—who happened to be present at the time of this experiment in Pavlov's laboratory in the Academy of Medicine—saw the changed behavior of the dog, he exclaimed: "Now I understand the joy with which the Christian martyrs went to the stake!"[4]

In the Christian experience, the hope God gives in Christ has the power to block fear. Hope's anticipation is so much greater than any fear the pain of this world can induce that

---

[4] O. Hobart Mowrer, *Learning Theory and Behavior* (New York: John Wiley & Sons, Inc., 1960), pp. 432-33.

courage is the inevitable result. Or, at least it should be that way. The magnificent exhortation of Hebrews 10:35 to 12: 29 begins with a recollection of hope's anticipation: "Cast not away therefore your confidence, which hath great recompense of reward. For ye have need of patience, that, after ye have done the will of God, ye might receive the promise" (10: 35-36). And Peter, who was himself an early martyr, expressed this dynamic of courage through anticipation of glory, born of hope:

> Blessed be the God and Father of our Lord Jesus Christ, which according to his abundant mercy hath begotten us again unto a lively hope by the resurrection of Jesus Christ from the dead, to an inheritance incorruptible, and undefiled, that fadeth not away, reserved in heaven for you, who are kept by the power of God through faith unto salvation ready to be revealed in the last time. Wherein ye greatly rejoice, though now for a season, if need be, ye are in heaviness through manifold temptations: that the trial of your faith, being much more precious than of gold that perisheth, though it be tried with fire, might be found unto praise and honour and glory at the appearing of Jesus Christ: whom having not seen, ye love; in whom, though now ye see him not, yet believing, ye rejoice with joy unspeakable and full of glory: receiving the end of your faith, even the salvation of your souls (1 Pet. 1:3-9).

So hope gives vitality, a new and dynamic life that expresses itself in action and courage.

## 2. Variety in Hope

Although hope's dynamics are predictable, hope's forms are not. Variety is a word that can describe the ways in which Christian hope has expressed itself since before Pentecost. One form of hope's expectation, beginning in the New Testament, could be called radical interventionism. This form of hope looks upon history as redeemable only through a supernatural interdiction. So the apostles, being patriotic Jews, despised the Roman's rule and all the injustices it spawned. They saw no real basis for hope in their present, expecting an intervention by the divine hand. With the resurrection of Jesus to quicken this hope, the fall of the usurping Roman authority seemed a light thing for their surprising God. Expecting him to reach out at any hour in an apocalyptic kind of turnover, they asked the inevitable question of Jesus: "Wilt thou at this time restore again the kingdom of Israel?" Acts 1:6).

But such interventionist hope was eventually tamed by the necessities of history. The church lived in anticipation of Christ's imminent second coming, but the lesson of adjustment was imposed upon them by Christ's delay. Economic irresponsibility, adopted under the guise of a fervent expression of hope, was condemned by the apostle Paul (2 Thess. 3:7-12). Cynics, who had fanned the flames of skepticism, using the delay of Christ's coming as a bellows to feed the fire, were roundly denounced (2 Pet. 3:3-9). The Hebrews epistle appears to have come to terms with this deferred hope and to counsel an interim stance of courage and the good witness of a consistent life (Heb. 13:12-21). The New Testament closes with Christians suffering under the heavy hand of Roman oppression, sustained only by the hope of Christ's return—a hope vividly communicated through the revelator's vision of the coming triumph God will give his own in Christ. And the witness, groaning under the burden of Christ's delay, closed his vision with the fervent prayer, "Even so, come, Lord Jesus" (Rev. 22:20).

For more than a long millennium, radical interventionism as a widespread form of hope waned, beginning with the close of the New Testament era. Perhaps this was the effect of the church-state coalition. But in the volatile sixteenth century, a new expression of radical interventionism broke out among the Anabaptists in central Europe. Hans Hut of southern Germany, Melchior Hoffmann of Friesland, and Jan Mathys, along with Jan Beukelssen of Holland, all preached an abrupt end to history in the very near future by the return of Christ. They organized communities of believers who, in some instances, set aside property rights, and the ordinary social and moral proprieties, in the expectation of an apocalyptic judgment through warfare, ending with Christ's return. Perhaps the most radical of these groups was that in Munster. Among those of Munster were defecting followers of Strasbourg's Melchior Hoffmann, whose prophecies of his own imprisonment were fulfilled, except for the duration. He had predicted, when imprisoned in 1533, that six months after would come the end of the world. However, by the time he died ten years later (and still in prison), the most fanatic of his followers had long since joined the Munster group where large numbers of radicals had gathered. In February, 1534, they gained the mastery of the city and drove out those who would not accept the new order. The bishop of Munster laid siege to the city. Mathys was killed in battle. Jan Beukelssen was proclaimed king. Polygamy was established, community of goods was enforced, all opponents bloodily put down. On June 24, 1935, the bishop (aided by Catholic and Lutheran troops) captured the city, and the leaders were put to death by extreme torture. Thoroughly discredited, such rampant radicalism was exposed for what it was: a gross distortion of the Christian hope.[5] Since then, the expectations of radical interventionists in the mainstream of Christian life have been tempered by the cautions of the New Testament, and the discretions taught by this bit of tragic history.

---

[5] For further reading on the chiliastic movements in the Reformation period, see W. W. Walker, *A History of the Christian Church* (New York: Chas. Scribner's Sons, 1945), pp. 366-75.

Another form taken by Christian hope, indicating its variety of forms, could be called the belief in inevitable progress. The idea originated outside the Christian community, although Christianity as a social force contributed to its beginnings. The date for this belief can be set in the first half of the eighteenth century, in that period of European history called the Age of Enlightenment. A generally optimistic outlook was combined with Rousseau's idea that man's capacity to reason was capable of indefinite perfection. The French philosopher had a name for his idea: *"La perfectibilite de le raison"* (the perfectibility of reason). The phrase was used, not only to describe a fact (according to him) which was observable in the life of the individual, but also in human life as a whole. Further, the phrase expressed his conviction that the increase in the power of reasoning and the knowledge gained thereby, along with the technologies such knowledge would produce, could not help but improve the conditions of human life.

In the nineteenth century, biological science (following Darwin's lead), and the psychological discipline (following the Freudian lead), further buttressed the idea of inevitable progress. This belief pervaded men's thoughts in every realm; politics, sciences, human behavior, education, business, even the life of the church.

But the prevailing optimism was brought up short by certain events of history. The war fought to end all wars ended in a broken dream called the League of Nations. The Second World War, the outgrowth of the tensions left from the First World War, ended in a brilliant burst of destructive power raining death upon the Japanese cities, Nagasaki and Hiroshima. Men learned slowly and painfully the hard lesson: progress in knowledge is not progress in moral force. Even now, the churches and denominations in America are learning to live with the harsh fact that Christian hope cannot be translated into statistical gains and strengthened institutions.

With a kind of glacial inevitability mankind as a whole is having to yield his dream of inevitable progress. The private man is coming to his own painful awareness of what a so-called progressive, cybernetic world can mean to his insides, as well as to the world he lives in. So Charles Malik, the Lebanese Christian diplomat, describes the contemporary moral scene:

> In the New Testament there are a dozen or more listings of the sins of that age. All those sins are rampant today. But we may add as peculiar to our age: driveness, nervousness, cowardice, rebelliousness, absence of rest and peace, flattening of thought and feeling, absence of the dimension of depth, innumerable new ways in which pleasure can be safely stolen, disintegration of community, massive irrationality and superstition, reliance upon speculation and chance, disdain of the law of cause and effect, weakening of the sense of personal responsibility, denial of the invisible and spiritual, the spread of militant atheism, the proud self-sufficiency of man.[6]

The idea of progress is not in the New Testament, nor was it in the mind of any of the New Testament writers so far as we can tell. We may mistake the New Testament's affirmation of the possibility of growing in Christlikeness as a form of progress. But progress depends upon developing that which is already latent within. Christlikeness is God's gift through his shaping, helping Spirit. Or we may take certain kingdom parables as teaching the idea of inevitable progress. However, those parables must be understood and interpreted with the sharp fact that Jesus taught that both tares and wheat would grow together until the harvest. Inevitable progress holds the vision of a field without tares, and cannot square with the plain teaching of Jesus nor the hard facts of

---

[6] "The Burden of the Christian," *The Christian Century*, December 20, 1961, p. 1524. Used by permission.

human experience. We must conclude that inevitable progress is a secularization of Christian hope, and only mimics
the true reality.[7]

Still another form of Christian hope can be seen in the efforts of certain contemporary scholars, reckoning with the
harsh realities of history, to limit the Christian hope, and
especially the blessed hope of Christ's second coming, to an
altogether personal and internal dimension. So Dr. Rudolf
Bultmann has established two canons for a "true" eschatology:
(1) It must not embody cosmological elements; and (2) it
must conform to historicity. However, by the first canon, Dr.
Bultmann has succeeded in establishing an eternal duality in
the cosmos; by the second he has compromised seriously
Christ's lordship over creation. Only a hope that embraces
the man and his world can be true to New Testament Christianity.[8]

One other form by which the Christian's hope has been
described through internal dimensions has been called "realized eschatology." Dr. C. H. Dodd of Cambridge, adhering
to the New Testament text and biblical thought patterns, sees
the Old Testament day of the Lord as declared to have happened in Christ. Emphasizing the gospel as fulfilment, in
that the supernatural has entered history, challenged the
powers of evil, judged the world, and made possible eternal
life in present experience, Dr. Dodd concludes that the New
Testament writers applied Jewish ideas of eschatology to the
coming of Jesus. So the Old Testament expectation has
passed into history and is "realized." However, Christians,
living in an "eschatological now," are governed still by the
bounds of finiteness. In that sense, and in the bondage of the

---

[7] For a full discussion of this distortion of Christian hope, see Emil
Brunner, *Faith, Hope, and Love* (Philadelphia: The Westminster Press,
1956), pp. 37-58.

[8] See Charles W. Kegley, *The Theology of Rudolf Bultmann* (New
York: Harper & Row, Publishers, 1966), pp. 65-82.

world to man's condition, the "ultimate finality" of Christ's coming has yet to be realized. Taking crisis as the clue for understanding history, and especially the concrete event of the incarnation in Christ's first coming, with its judgment of sin and triumph over death, Dr. Dodd concludes: "The goal of history is that which moulds itself upon the great divine event of the past, known in its concrete actuality, and depicts its final issue in a form which brings time to an end and places man in eternity—the second coming of the Lord, the last judgment."[9]

Beyond the variety of forms Christian hope takes, of which we have surveyed but a few, is the fact of the hope itself: God through Christ assuring his own ultimate purpose for man, in man's history, and embracing man's world, through the coming of Christ to earth a second time, thus completing what was begun at his first coming.

### 3. Hope's Creativity

We have noted here hope's vitality and hope's variety. There remains hope's creativity. By that is meant hope's power to create in men a dynamic, new response to their present; to their here and now. For this purpose, let us turn to the days immediately after Pentecost, and in the New Testament church.

Perhaps we need to recall that the church was a community of hope, created by the fact of the resurrection. (See chap. 1.) Now the hope vibrant in the church of the New Testament created certain expectations, extending in a horizontal direction. The members of the Jerusalem fellowship hoped to be participants in a radically new kind of community in which an even-handed impartiality would be the hallmark. Apparently that expectation—which was a hope concerning

---

⁹ C. H. Dodd, *The Apostolic Preaching and Its Developments* (London: Hodder & Stoughton, Ltd., 1951), pp. 79-96.

the quality of the interpersonal relationships they would experience—was disappointed. The Grecian widows began to
murmur . . . an interesting word. In this highly charged
spiritual atmosphere, tensions created by hope did not de-
crease; they increased. So what happened? The Spirit, who
had created the expectation, helped the members in the
creation of a new form: a distinctive lay office. Many see in
the account of this incident the beginning of the diaconate.
But whatever it may have been, this we know: the new form
—that new order—gave the church Stephen and Philip. Philip
became an effective evangelist—possibly helped by the new
status invested in him by his lay office. Stephen became an
effective witness, and the first martyr.

In this development we see the creative power of hope at
work in the community of hope. But the creative dynamism
is only begun in that community. While the new form of lay
recognition was being formed, the church was under inner
stress toward further expansion and inclusiveness. One cannot
help but be surprised to discover the crisscrossing of kinship
and friendship lines among the earliest followers of Jesus.
Those gathered in the upper room comprised a small circle
of friends, acquaintances, and kinsmen—almost a family affair.
But when Pentecost came, the closed-in fellowship exploded
under the creative dynamism of the hope it proclaimed. The
converts of Pentecost read like a United Nations of the first-
century Mediterranean world. The seeds sown in Jerusalem
were to flower in places as far away as Rome and North
Africa. Narrow Jewish concerns were doomed; hope in Christ
had created larger horizons. Caesarea, Antioch, the mission-
ary expansion under Paul and Barnabas, the intrusion of the
gospel into the households of the Caesars—these were natural
developments to creative hope. The hope that Christ gives
cannot be contained in the old forms, the old assumptions,
or any old status quo that denies the fulness of his gospel.
Christian hope creates new forms, new scope, and in the

process helps resolve old tensions and settle old antipathies. Christian hope was given of God to challenge what is, with what ought to be in Christ. For this kind of hope has, among its many biblical shapes, the shape of expectation.

But a community—even a community of hope—is made up of individuals. What dynamism operative on the individuals making up the community of hope creates this distinctive tone of which we have taken notice? Perhaps it was given to the writer of 1 John to spell out one aspect of that dynamism we have not yet named. When we read John, we wonder why his truth had not already occurred to us. Do you recall 3:3: "And every man that hath this hope in him purifieth himself, even as he is pure?"

Perhaps we can see this dynamic of creative hope better obliquely. Not long ago, I learned the meaning of the word "fletcher." A fletcher was the man who, after slitting the arrows, attached their tail feathers. The significance of his task was this: the fletching, if properly done, became a kind of surrogate mind that took over for man while the arrow was in flight. Fletching was a primitive way of installing an in-flight guidance system. The fletching kept the arrow moving toward its target.

Hope is the Christian's fletcher. If he has hope, that hope is the gift of God's pure Christ. The Christian holds the vision of the pure Christ before him, and by that vision Christ becomes the definition of what the Christian himself is to become by God's grace. Hope helps him move toward his target: becoming like Christ. In that aspect of hope's creative energy is the explanation of lives likes Augustine, Francis of Assissi, Bernard of Clairvaux, Albert Schweitzer, William Wallace—and yourself?

We began this chapter by taking note of one contemporary writer's description of modern man's loss of nerve; his prevailing sense of anxiety, if not fear. One mode of anticipating the future is anxiety—the chronic condition that cankers and corrodes life. Another mode of anticipating the future is fear—the condition that magnifies anxiety into crisis. However, there is another mode of anticipating the future. That mode is Christian hope. In such hope there is neither anxiety nor fear as the dominant mood. For the Christian's hope includes the blessed hope of Christ's coming again. And in his coming, the future can only bring to us that toward which we hopefully and expectantly move.